# TACKLING COMPLEXITY

# TACKLING COMPLEXITY

**TOUGH-LOVE INTERACTIONS TO NAVIGATE UNCERTAINTY, PROMOTE POSITIVITY, AND DELIVER PERFORMANCE EXCELLENCE**

ANU RATHNINDE

Copyright © 2022 Anu Rathninde
All rights reserved. No part of this publication may be reproduced, distributed, or transmitted in any form or by any means, including photocopying, recording, or other electronic or mechanical methods, without the prior written permission of the publisher, except in the case of brief quotations embodied in critical reviews and certain other noncommercial uses permitted by copyright law.

Contact information for S-IILA Business – www.s-iila.com

ISBN: 978-981-18-2588-0 (print)
ISBN: 978-981-18-2589-7 (ebook)

Ordering Information:
Special discounts are available on quantity purchases by corporations, associations, and others. For details, contact www.s-iila.com.

## *Dedication*

*This book is dedicated to leaders at all levels who are continuing to learn and adapt to become better leaders and, frankly, live better lives.*

# TABLE OF CONTENTS

Introduction . . . . . . . . . . . . . . . . . . . . . . 1
    The Accountability Secret                             3
    About Me                                                   4
    The SIILA Model                                           5

## PART I: COMPLEXITY

**Chapter 1: Why Leaders Fail** . . . . . . . . . . . . . . . . . 11
    Newtonian Paradigm and Deterministic Leadership         15
    Statistical Paradigm and Average Leadership              18
**Chapter 2: What Is Complexity and Why Do You Need to Care** . . . . . 21
    No User Manual                                            21
    Running on Shifting Landscapes                         23
    Complex Adaptive Systems                              25
    Everyday Scenarios                                     26
    Boeing: The 737 MAX Complexity                        27
    On Becoming a Complexity Leader                      31
    SIILA Model with Tough-Love Interactions in Tackling Complexity    34

## PART II: SYSTEMS THINKING

### Chapter 3: How the Boardroom and Shop Floor Are Connected . . . . . 41
    Organizational Interconnectivity      44
    Organizational Disconnect      47
    Mingling Around the Corners      48
    Why Is the Leader Held Responsible for Everything?      49
    Easier Said Than Done      50
    Leadership Responsibility Model      52

### Chapter 4: Your Organization Has a Mind and Life of Its Own . . . . . 57
    Emergence      58
    Making the Grass Greener on Your Side      61
    Creating Positive Emergence      63
    Eliminating Negative Emergence      64

## PART III: INTERNALIZE

### Chapter 5: Why You Need to Know What's Driving You . . . . . . . . 69
    The Power of the Mind      70
    The Psychological Mind of Bad Leadership      74
    Why Do You Want to Be a Leader?      76

### Chapter 6: Power of Mastering Yourself. . . . . . . . . . . . . . 79
    Why Do You Want to Know Yourself?      80
    Self-Leadership      82
    Good Values for a Leader      85

## PART IV: INTERACT

### Chapter 7: Why Tough-Love Interactions Are Worth More Than Gold . . 91
    Leadership as a Conversation      93
    Intentions      97
    Consistency      97
    Interactions      98
    Intimacy      98
    Confronting the Brutal Realities      99

Chapter 8: Know Who's Really on Your Team . . . . . . . . . . . **103**
    Forgive but Never Forget      107
    Telescoping Behavior and Performance      107
    Lead with a Healthy Image      109

Chapter 9: How to Break Down Silos and Build Up Teams . . . . . . **111**
    Clarity of Purpose      112
    Weak Links in the Supply Chain      114
    Broken Windows Theory      116
    Escalation Business School      117

## PART V: LEARN

Chapter 10: How Leaders Begin to Learn with Tough-Love
    Interactions . . . . . . . . . . . . . . . . . **125**
    Technical Knowledge Gap      126
    Organization Knowledge Gap      130
    Get Small Things Right      132

Chapter 11: Your Leadership Is Tested on This One Step . . . . . . . **135**
    The Power of Teaching to Learn and Influence      136
    What Is Teachable Point of View?      139
    Be Here Now      141
    What Is Your Teachable Point of View?      144
    You, Your Job, and Your Career      145

## PART VI: ADAPT

Chapter 12: It's Not the Knowledge ... It's What You Do with It . . . **151**
    Why Can't Leaders Change Themselves?      154
    Why Is Change So Hard?      157
    Individual Change Profile      157

Chapter 13: Reinventing Better Versions . . . . . . . . . . . . **161**
    Reinventing Yourself      163
    How Leaders Change Organizations      165
    The Leader Embraces the SIILA Model      167

## PART VII: SIILA JOURNEY

**Chapter 14: The SIILA Loop Never Ends—Turn Knowledge into Skills into Habits** . . . . . . . . . . . . . . . . . . . . . 171
- Leadership Is Forming New Habits — 172
- On Becoming Unconsciously Competent — 174
- SIILA Is a Habit — 176

**Chapter 15: My SIILA Journey** . . . . . . . . . . . . . . . . . . . 181
- That Coconut Tree and Lessons from My Parents — 182
- Model What You Know — 184
- My Failures and Cycles of Learning — 185
- Capitalize on Your Past — 185
- Lifelong Learning in Leadership — 189

**Endnotes** . . . . . . . . . . . . . . . . . . . . . . . . 191
**Acknowledgments** . . . . . . . . . . . . . . . . . . . 201
**Index** . . . . . . . . . . . . . . . . . . . . . . . . . . 209

# INTRODUCTION

It is time for leaders to embrace complexity.

For the last century, leaders have tried to simplify the inherent chaos and complexity as they oversee real people. They've tried to pull certain "levers" in an organization to get a desired outcome, treating human beings like machines. But there's a very real problem with that approach.

People are not machines. Organizations are not machines. They are living things. And like all living things, they change, respond, adapt, grow, and evolve every day. No one can stop it. When you instead embrace complexity, you can make it work *for* you rather than *against* you.

Despite the complexities of the environment in which we operate today, middle- to senior-level leaders are under tremendous pressure to get things done and deliver on their commitments—even when the outcome is uncertain.

Leaders often jump into new jobs and develop a plan for the organization in 30 days. Senior management gets help from advisers and typically communicates the new strategy in an off-site meeting, using the latest industry buzzwords to get people excited.

There's nothing wrong with that approach. Leaders do, after all, have to have the ability to envision the future and develop an appropriate strategy to make that future a reality.

## TACKLING COMPLEXITY

The real challenge lies in getting things done. All too often, these plans fail to deliver the outcomes the leader committed to. When the plans fail, too many leaders blame anyone and anything, from the employees to the culture, to the customers, to the suppliers, to the government, to the investors, to the market—and eventually get fired.

Leaders fool themselves into thinking they can expect their plans to work if they just "pull the right lever" or if they just understand the right things.

Many leaders today don't understand complexity.

The reality is you never know the secret of making your people and your organization work exactly the way you plan. Even if you find out that secret, by the time you figure it out, it's already changed. That's complexity.

People, organizations, customers, suppliers, and the market all interact with each other all the time. They are interdependent. They learn from each other and evolve continuously.

If a leader expects an organization to operate like a machine and the plan to work exactly as it has been communicated, he must be prepared to fail. And when he does, he must plan to be held accountable for that failure. Leaders are held accountable for everything that goes on in the organization, even if it seems, at times, to be uncontrollable.

Throughout this book, we'll examine leaders such as Boeing's CEO, Dennis Muilenburg, who developed a plan to reduce costs, improve margins, and expedite Boeing's new 737 MAX aircraft launch. It was a great plan, and share prices went up. The new aircraft was launched, but it was soon revealed the engineers cut corners to meet the leader's demands. Engineers did not build the necessary redundancies into the MAX control systems but should have. As a result of a single malfunctioning sensor, two deadly plane crashes happened just four months apart. Hundreds of people were killed. The company paid billions of dollars in penalties, technical fixings, legal fees, and compensation. Those expenses don't even factor in the cost of reputation loss.

The results Muilenburg promised were not delivered, and he lost his job.

## THE ACCOUNTABILITY SECRET

As a leader, you may feel that it's not your responsibility if one junior engineer designed a poor-quality product or that it's not something you can manage. But if you think getting quality products and services out of your people and your factory on time at the right cost and quality is too low-level of a task for you, you will fail.

A leader must find a way to get things done in all corners of the organization. It's not the plan itself that will get things done. It's what you do as a leader every day that will help the organization achieve its goals. When leaders embrace complexity, they will focus on the simple things that matter most.

The moment a leader starts thinking that it's someone else's problem or someone else's fault when things go wrong, the problems can only get worse. Leaders might not only lose their jobs, but they might lose themselves morally and psychologically in the process.

Being accountable for your own ability to become better is the key to continuous success. That's why a leader's mindset is the starting point of success. It cannot be delegated. It starts with you.

Leaders are expected to deliver results again and again. It's not about their average performance. It's about superior performance every time. People might be able to fake success for a while—maybe even for a big project or two—but they won't be able to replicate this caliber of success without the right mindset.

A leader's mindset is reflected in how the leader thinks, behaves, and learns every day. A leader has the right mindset when they balance their focus on people and results, short-term success and long-term success.

The secret to tackling complexity and getting things done is a leader's ability to influence the organization so that it emerges positively.

Leaders who understand that need will be able to deliver their performance unconsciously. It becomes a habit ingrained in how they live their lives and perform even basic tasks.

There is no shortage of literature in leadership disciplines, from having a great vision, to developing a strategy, to building a great team, to being a good communicator, to developing your people, advising on how to get things done. But being good at any one of those aspects doesn't ensure leaders will be able to get the job done and deliver on the expectations.

If a leader is too focused on results, good people eventually leave and the organization fails. If a leader is too focused on its people and cares nothing for the results, a company will become bankrupt, and the organization will still fail.

The same thing happens if a leader is too focused on long-term innovations. If they lose sight of short-term priorities, problems build up and the organization collapses. If a leader is too focused on the short term, the company never grows or develops or tackles larger issues.

It's time for leaders to embrace complexity. Most leaders understand that the outcome in any complex situation is uncertain—yet leaders still use methods and practices that rely on that certainty. That will not make the cut.

## ABOUT ME

I have been successful in leading large organizations in Asia, North America, and Europe for over 25 years. I studied leadership in Asia, North America, and Europe as well. I became very interested in finding out why some leaders were successful with everything they did and made leadership look easy, while others made leadership seem like a dangerous place to be, destined to fail.

That curiosity led me to research leadership.

INTRODUCTION

I concluded that the ability of a leader to tackle complexity comes down to their mindset and the need to get the small things right, especially those that matter most—in life and at work.

It comes down to what the leader does every day, every moment, that will differentiate whether they get things done and deliver on expectations or fail. If a leader can't get the little things right, there is no chance of getting big things done.

In this book, I offer the best of my own hands-on leadership experience and academic research. I have seen firsthand how leaders in Eastern and Western countries approach leadership. This book is an attempt to bridge these two styles. After decades of study, both academic and hands-on, I've come to the conclusion that great leaders employ the best practices from both worlds. It is about leveraging the best of the ancient Asian wisdom and modern science.

## THE SIILA MODEL

This seven-part book will present the systems thinking, internalize, interact, learn, and adapt sections in the SIILA model, which will teach leaders how to tackle complexity and get things done when the outcome is uncertain in the knowledge era.

**Part I: chapters 1 and 2** explain how the age of determinism has ended, and therefore outcomes are uncertain. When the outcomes are uncertain, the statistical paradigm makes us use statistically significant solutions. But these solutions aren't good enough to tackle complexities and deliver results consistently. Leaders must embrace complexity. People, organizations, and markets all are living things that continue to evolve, even without a leader, which makes organizations complex adaptive systems (CAS), as we will discuss. The five-step SIILA model is the way to tackle complexity and get things done.

**Part II: chapters 3 and 4** cover *systems thinking*. That step explains the interconnectedness and interdependencies within an organization and explains why leaders are held accountable for everything that happens. Part II also describes how and why organizations emerge positively to get things done or with negativity, which leads to failure. Leaders can't stop organizational emergence—much like a parent can't stop a child from growing up—but they can influence it so it emerges positively.

**Part III: chapters 5 and 6** cover *internalize*, which refers to the attitudes and behaviors that influence a leader to unconsciously do the right thing. This part of the book explains the power of the mind to influence positive emergence. It also explains the power of mastering yourself and self-leadership as the starting point. This section will encourage you to confront yourself and discover your true motivations so that you can identify bad habits and remove them in order to learn new, good habits.

**Part IV: chapters 7, 8, and 9** cover *interactions* within and outside the organization at all levels. Leaders often get too much good news only and are protected by the people around them, so they never get to know the truth. To know the truth, leaders must get out, go see, and interact with all corners of the organization. That practice is how leaders learn about the people working for them and the status of the organization. This part of the book will explain how learning about the culture, capabilities, and capacities of an organization in a hands-on, cross-functional way can lead to effective issue resolution that increases productivity.

**Part V: chapters 10 and 11** cover how leaders *learn* from their interactions. Leaders typically have two kinds of knowledge gaps. The first is technical knowledge, which revolves around the products, systems, and processes of the organization. The second is the organizational knowledge gap, which involves the real culture, capabilities, capacities, and direction of the organization under the leader. Great leaders are great teachers. They teach in order to learn about the people working for them. Leaders can use teaching as the way to validate their own teachable point of view and leadership point of view while continuing to help influence the organization to move toward the direction they expect.

**Part VI: chapters 12 and 13** cover how leaders *adapt* after they learn. Learning has no meaning unless it is applied to a real-life practical situation and becomes a skill. These chapters discuss why some leaders find it so hard to change themselves and show leaders how they can identify their self-change profile to get them started.

**Part VII: chapter 14** covers why leaders must pay attention to what they do every day and why the small things matter. By the time a leader learns about the organization, it changes. The only way to keep up is to make learning itself a habit. That's why leaders must go on this *never-ending SIILA loop* of systems thinking, internalize, interact, learn, and adapt. By making SIILA a habit, leaders can get things done by tackling complexity with tough-love interactions when the outcome is uncertain in the knowledge era.

**Chapter 15** shares my own SIILA journey. Leadership requires lifelong learning. It's not a debate about whether leaders are born or made: It's about leaders continuing to learn and adapt that makes the difference. It's a stage when you embrace complexity, and your mind unconsciously focuses on the small things that matter most every time.

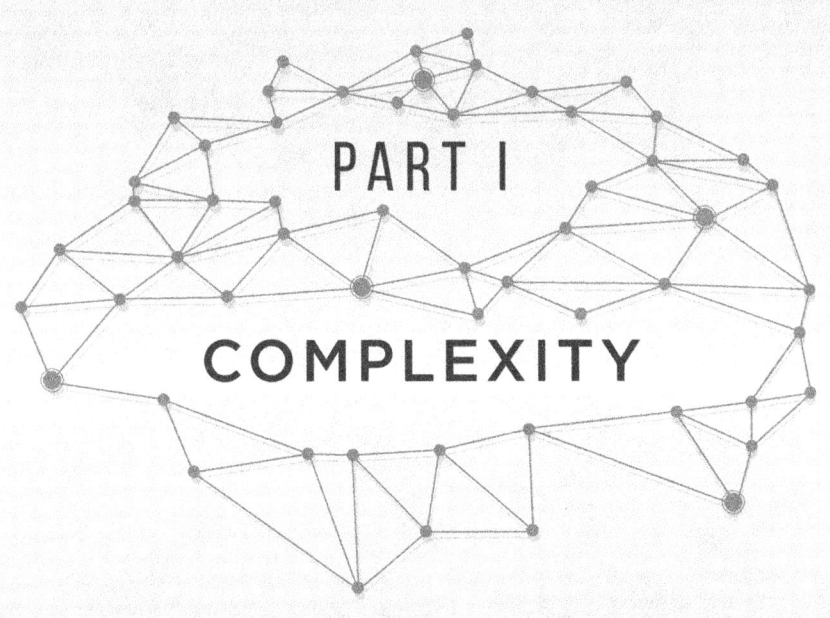

# PART I
# COMPLEXITY

# CHAPTER 1

# WHY LEADERS FAIL

Leaders are under tremendous pressure to get things done. With stakeholders from investors to community members watching a leader's every move, leaders are expected to deliver exactly what they promised. This pressure won't change. In fact, it will only become more intense moving forward.

Most CEOs, presidents, general managers, functional leaders, project managers, and other leaders will tell you that meeting their performance targets and getting things done is of the utmost importance to them. They have a plan. Maybe it's ambitious but still reasonable in their minds, and stakeholders expect leaders to deliver on these commitments.

Yet so often the organization falls short of those expectations. Now, those organizations and the leaders themselves have to deal with the consequences.

When an organization hires a new leader—whether a new CEO, general manager, or a project manager—the hiring manager celebrates. The choice is seen as a chance for the leader to prove themselves. The newly hired leader typically gets the freedom to do what he or she wants in order to deliver results. Such liberty may mean hiring their own team, firing those who don't make the cut, executing new strategies, making new investment decisions, and even making a cultural transformation.

In this example, the hiring manager assumed that after hiring the new leader, they would see the expected results. But the hiring manager was wrong in that assumption.

Similar to the hiring manager, the new leader celebrates getting the job and hopes to build a new career. They usually make many changes in the organization, choosing to hire people, fire people, and deploy new strategies. They think by doing the same thing they did before, they will get the same results.

But so often, leaders fail to fulfill their promises. Not only do they fall short of the expectations they agreed to meet, but the organization is actually worse off than before.

This is the failure of determinism: decisions are made with a belief that they are the "right" decisions, but they could very easily turn out to be the wrong decisions for the situation at hand.

You will find various definitions and interpretations on determinism, but the crux of it is this: expecting the same exact actions to deliver the same exact results to create the expected outcome. Such thinking minimizes the very important role that responsibility and self-control play in real life.

Let's look at another example.

In January 2020, all leaders started the new year with committed business plans in hand, five-year strategic goals identified, and travel plans set for the year. Then-U.S. President Donald Trump was preparing to run for his second term, pointing to the United States' booming economy as proof of a successful first term.

But soon the COVID-19 pandemic disrupted those plans. The world came to a standstill. Almost all business plans fell far short of their original plans, and Donald Trump lost the presidential election.

Many businesses were tempted to blame the pandemic for these issues. But although many problems were and are intertwined with the pandemic, not every loss was or is caused by it.

For example, in 2021, a global semiconductor chip shortage was positioned to affect millions of people worldwide. The chips are critical in a variety of technologies from cars, to televisions, to toothbrushes. Poor management of supply chain capacity created massive disruptions to the global industrial output.[1] The real reason is poor leadership. The product application rate in the market and the capacity planning—all the way down to the lowest tier in the supply chain—were not connected.

Two of the world's biggest aircraft manufacturers also made some gigantic mistakes on their iconic new product launches. Ultimately, they didn't launch the new aircraft on time with the expected quality and associated financial performance. Many companies in the value chain lost money, and people lost their jobs.

In 2019, the European manufacturer Airbus had already stopped its production of the superjumbo jet A380 after one of its biggest buyers, Emirates Airlines, cut its order.

Announcing the decision to stop building A380 superjumbo aircraft, then-CEO of Airbus, Tom Enders, said there was no basis to sustain the production and that the decision to stop production was painful. Analysts estimated that project cost over $25 billion.[2] Delivery was delayed several years due to quality and supply chain issues, and only some 200 plus aircrafts were delivered, while the target was over 1,200.[3] Talk about a significant failure!

Similarly, Boeing's 787 Dreamliner also faced an expensive, delayed launch and quality issues to the tune of billions above the project budget. Boeing's 787 was originally scheduled to be launched in 2008 but did not start deliveries until 2011. Even after the delayed launch, the aircraft had a number of large problems from fuel leaks, to smoke in the cabin, to fires.

In both cases, the companies did not deliver on their commitments. Leaders across the multitier supply chain lost money and jobs, and the shareholder value was reduced.

It's worth noting that these are great companies with smart leaders, excellent risk-mitigation plans, nearly unlimited resources, and multiple layers of reviews. Yet, those CEOs didn't deliver the outcomes that stakeholders expected at the outset of the project. But it's not just the CEOs. It's all the leaders—divisional and business unit presidents, functional leaders, project managers, manufacturing plant managers, and those who make such commitments at all levels. Sure, they didn't plan to fail. But they did.

So, why do so many leaders fall from grace?

Many leaders will talk about how much they have grown the business, improved profitability, or fixed broken operations, all while showing beautiful, shiny new charts showcasing their plans and commitments. But when the rubber meets the road, they often fail to deliver on what they promised or committed to.

Why?

It's impossible to predict the outcomes they claim, so the results they commit to are just as risky.

When those planned outcomes don't materialize, whether that's the company's profit growth or a new product launch, leaders often blame anything from suppliers, to policies, to bosses, to employees, to customers, and more. Then, they usually get fired.

Despite many interviews, thorough background checks, and in-depth psychological evaluations, such leaders still failed to deliver.

Leaders primarily get hired into jobs based on past success, under the rationale that because they were successful in the past, they will be successful again. The underpinning is the principle of strong causation. But past success doesn't guarantee future success.

It's important to realize that the principle of strong causation is not valid for today's businesses. There are too many variables at play, and these variables keep changing.

Nevertheless, here is the starting point that will address the situation and its challenges.

Leaders today must understand and accept that the outcome is uncertain. Today's business environment demands it, and it makes all the difference in how leaders approach their business commitments. Leaders must be willing to change their behaviors, methods, styles, and tactics to adapt to today's reality.

Before we get deeper into how leaders can accomplish it, let's find out why so many leaders still believe that if they follow their plan, they'll get the exact outcome they expect.

## NEWTONIAN PARADIGM AND DETERMINISTIC LEADERSHIP

As society shifted into the Industrial Revolution, people who previously worked on farms started working at factories. The owners of these factories saw workers strictly as laborers and looked for ways to better manage people.

Fredrick Taylor, a mechanical engineer by trade, wrote a book, *The Principles of Scientific Management,* in 1911.[4] Taylor became the father of scientific management.[5]

As a mechanical engineer, Taylor had mastered how machines work, which naturally influenced the way he understood the world. With that knowledge, he developed appropriate ways that worked at that time for managing people. He applied Newton's laws of motion to people, in the sense that the location and speed of any object can be perfectly determined to everyday life, so that one will generally be able to predict the outcome of another's actions.

Taylor's applications of Newton's determinism led to the concept that by "pulling the right levers" in the organization, leaders could get the outcome they expect to achieve. The theory essentially meant treating organizations as machines made up of laborers. With that awareness, the outcome was certain and predictable.

The Newtonian paradigm of determinism, coupled with the principle of strong causation, makes leaders believe whatever worked in one situation will work in another situation.

With this notion, countless leadership theories were born. Here's a sampling:

Leadership theories in the industrial age started with the great man theory,[6] which states leaders are born to lead, and traits theory,[7] which assumes that people inherit certain qualities and traits that make them better suited for leadership. Both theories assume leaders are born rather than made.

In the 1940s, leadership researchers began to switch gears, stating that anyone could be made a leader if they learned the appropriate response to any given situation. It became known as the behavioral leadership theory,[8] which gave rise to teaching leadership, especially in business schools.

Another theory that was developed later is the transactional leadership theory,[9] which essentially suggests that leaders can get the most out of their followers by rewarding good work and punishing poor work until the problem is corrected. You'll likely find this leadership model in military boot camps. In a business setting, the practice would look like paying people for good work, while firing people for bad work. It's based on the idea that employees are not self-motivated and require constant monitoring and instruction to get the job done.

The idea of control-based leadership is accepted as the norm. In this model, leaders are seen as authority figures who have the ultimate say in how things go.

On the other hand, the contingency leadership theory suggests that there is no single best style of leadership.[10] The best leaders are those who know how to adopt different styles of leadership in different situations. These leaders know that just because one approach to leadership worked well in the past does not mean that it will work again when the situation changes. You can observe how determinism and the principle of strong causation have started to lose their place in leadership practices.

Although there's no shortage of leadership theories, another is transformation leadership theory, and it is important that we also touch base on it. In the transformational leadership theory, a charismatic leader motivates the members of the organization to transcend their self-interests in order to achieve collective objectives.[11]

Those theories, even if at the later stages wherein some human aspects become integrated, are still built around the premise that an organization can be viewed as a machine for leaders to use to get done what they want. They assume that if they tweak one variable, they will get the result they are looking for.

That approach worked better during the industrial age, when resources seemed to be unlimited, labor seemed to be interchangeable, and organizations didn't need to use any employee's knowledge or learning capacity to stay competitive.

That just won't cut it today.

As the industrial age becomes a distant memory, we must embrace our transition to the knowledge era to truly understand what makes a company succeed or fail. In the knowledge era, the competitive advantage is predicated on the knowledge it has and social aspects it masters. Thus, the learning capacity of a firm becomes more valuable than its physical assets.

That determination means abandoning our long-held belief that you can treat an organization like a machine.

Instead, think of it like an organism.

With this understanding, leaders accept that the outcome is uncertain. They behave as if the outcome depends on what actions the leader takes to *influence* rather than control. The bureaucratic and control leadership has lost its dominance.

We've shifted from the industrial age to the knowledge era,[12] whether leaders today want to accept it or not. In this new era, knowledge—and knowing how to use it—is more valuable than labor; intellect is more valuable than material; ideas are more valuable than capital.

When you think wealth creation, think human imagination.

If the most important achievement of management in the twentieth century was to increase manual-worker productivity, as suggested by the well-known, influential management thinker Peter Drucker, the most important accomplishment in the twenty-first century will be to increase knowledge-worker productivity.[13] There are different methods involved when it comes to increasing the productivity of knowledge workers versus increasing the productivity of manual workers.

Leading organizations where knowledge is more important than labor, people are well informed with increased education, and the free flow of information is becoming harder and harder. Many books are available that state industrial age leadership does not work for the knowledge era that we live in today. But it is still in practice because it's easy to teach industrial age leadership. It's mechanical—it's easy to teach and easy to learn. Practicality, however, doesn't mean it works.

If industrial age leadership theories are not working in the knowledge era, why would leaders still practice them?

Because we don't know better.

## STATISTICAL PARADIGM AND AVERAGE LEADERSHIP

We keep doing the same thing and making the same mistakes. We realize it doesn't work, but we don't know what else to do, so we fall back on the same old theories and practices.

And it's no wonder because, in a sense, these theories "work," statistically speaking.

On average, these leadership theories produce results. But what does that mean? If 10 people buy stocks, six make money, and four end up on the streets, were the results really fruitful? But imagine here that when many people lose money in the stock market, it has long-term consequences in society. In this new era, we need to consider how each person matters and how each person is a resource. People are not machines, and those four who ended up on the streets in this example shouldn't be discarded. We are no longer operating in a winner-takes-all world.

The principle of strong causation is no longer relevant. It is replaced with the principle of weak causation that states on average the same input will create the same output. It is the beginning of the shift into the statistical paradigm. The end of determinism and the end of the principle of strong causation means we can no longer predict the certain outcome. So, the world shifted to study and apply methods that work with statistical significance.

To put it another way, it's like saying it's acceptable for a company to have an average executive turnover of 10%. Although the number may seem small and manageable, that turnover rate could have a massive impact depending on who leaves and who stays. The effect could be the difference between an organization that moves forward or an organization that moves backward. In this case, statistics can't tell us the whole story.

The same idea applies to leaders who have been successful in the past. Companies often hire leaders and expect them to produce the same results in a different situation.

But the conversations around average performance can be painful. If you do 10 things and you get six of them right, that can make you a hero in some circumstances. However, if you are the president of a company who is leading 10 businesses and six of them are successful, that means four of them failed. If you don't deliver in your current role, despite even some significant accomplishments, you will likely lose your job. It's not about statistics. It's about consistently delivering on commitments time and time again.

We don't have the tools to analyze weak causation or to analyze the inability to lead real-world businesses in the knowledge era. The reason is because organizations are not machines. One can't simply measure a couple numbers and predict the outcome. Labor is no longer the currency of the organizations—knowledge is. Today's leaders are expected to deliver performance even with uncertainty around learning, innovation, instability, globalization, and more. But the way most of us do business, by treating organizations as machines, won't get us there. As leaders in the knowledge era, we must begin to treat organizations like living things that continuously evolve and adapt—with or without a leader.

Living things such as people, organizations, markets, societies, and even rain forests all have the ability to interact, be interdependent, learn, and evolve. That ability is the definition of complexity. It is very different from a jet engine or a Swiss watch in which very many nonliving, mechanical components work together to form a complicated machine. Machines are complicated, but they don't evolve. Living things do. People and the organizations of which they are a part are living things, and therefore they are complex.

Enter the complexity paradigm. Leaders need to tackle complexity to get things done. In this book, you'll learn how to become a complexity leader to ensure your business will thrive well into the future. You'll learn how to shift your leadership style in a practical way so you can get things done even if the outcome is uncertain and even if the organization continues to adapt and evolve.

# CHAPTER 2

# WHAT IS COMPLEXITY AND WHY DO YOU NEED TO CARE

If a tire falls off a car—no matter how fancy the car is—you can't drive it. It's essentially nonfunctional. A mechanic can fix the tire, and the car will work again. If a gear gets jammed in a Swiss mechanical watch, it, too, will be nonfunctional until it's repaired. Neither of these complicated machines can fix themselves, but once fixed by a mechanic who follows the user manual, they can go back to working as they used to.

You can fix complicated machines. But complex systems are different.

## NO USER MANUAL

On May 25, 2020, George Perry Floyd Jr., a Black man, was murdered by a police officer in Minneapolis, USA, during an arrest after a store clerk suspected Floyd may have used a counterfeit $20 bill to buy cigarettes.

During the encounter, police officer Derek Chauvin, a White man, knelt on Floyd's neck for more than nine minutes as Floyd lay on the ground, facedown and handcuffed.

Chauvin was later convicted of second-degree unintentional murder, second-degree manslaughter, and third-degree murder. He was sentenced to 22.5 years in prison.[14]

At the same time, still suffering from the COVID-19 pandemic and unemployment levels not seen since the great recession,[15] many businesses in cities across the United States had to close as weeks of protest and civil unrest broke out in support of Floyd.

These are complex issues. They cannot be fixed by following a user manual. This is the complexity that today's leaders need to address in order to make progress and get things done.

In complex problems, a leader's reaction is paramount. It is akin to what happens when the board hires a bad CEO or fires a good CEO. We've seen what happens when a business gets a bad president, or a leader makes the wrong decision. The organization reacts.

Unlike living entities, when a tire falls off a car or the gear breaks in a watch, they simply rest, unused, until they are fixed by the mechanic. But when something happens to society, organizations, or the rain forest, they don't stand still. They don't wait until they're fixed. No mechanic can fix those problems; no user manual exists. Leaders will struggle unless they are willing to tackle this complexity.

The same can be said about people. People interact with each other. They are interdependent; they learn, adapt, and continue to evolve together. When George Floyd died, society was not quiet. Some people and ideas—such as the idea to defund police—rose into the local and national sphere but wouldn't have gained traction otherwise. In many cases, traditional, formal organization leaders lost control.

WHAT IS COMPLEXITY AND WHY DO YOU NEED TO CARE

## RUNNING ON SHIFTING LANDSCAPES

Jack Welch created one of the world's largest companies, General Electric, to which all other companies aspired. He led the company for 20 years as its CEO.[16] Growing revenue from $25 billion to $130 billion and profits from $1.5 billion to $15 billion, Jack Welch is celebrated as a legendary CEO, regarded by many as the greatest leader in his era.[17]

What happened after Jack retired?

The next CEO of General Electric, Jeff Immelt, lost billions of dollars in value. The company wasn't positioned to adapt well to the modern era. Neither was its leadership.

But in recent years, people have been examining General Electric's leadership more critically. Jack Welch relentlessly pushed for growth, but there was an arrogance around the idea of success—an arrogance that killed the company under his successor. General Electric is now known as one of the biggest business failures in American history.

I would argue that nothing is built to last, especially organizations. If Jack Welch was the greatest CEO of the century, why couldn't he build General Electric to last and succeed after his leadership? Jack Welch was able to deliver during his time as the CEO. Once the leadership changed, so did the organization.

Everyone talks about the arrogance that contributed to the failure of General Electric. And it's easy to blame the new leadership, because the failure happened after Jack Welch retired. The new leadership thought that because the company had been successful, it would continue to be successful.

Although the landscape is constantly changing, leaders can't blame those changes for their failures. They still have to perform. The organization changed when it changed hands from Welch to Immelt, even if everything else was the same. The environment around the organization changed. That's not inherently bad, but new leadership must embrace this complexity. Unless organizations are built to continue to learn and adapt, and leaders continue to learn and adapt, Welch-to-Immelt-type leadership transitions will continue to destroy successful organizations.

General Electric is an example of a company that didn't pivot well. Toyota, on the other hand, is an example of a company that has, so far, continued to be successful with many leadership changes along the way.

Toyota started off as a company making sewing machines before it began making cars.[18] Since then, it has built a reputation for being a strong company building quality products. It has even earned a reputation for working well with other companies in the supply chain.

After a major earthquake and tsunami affected Japan in 2011, after which Toyota's production fell 78% year over year, the company worked to better understand the supply chain in its entirety so it could cushion itself from potential impacts. Because of this new strategy, Toyota was largely insulated from the semiconductor shortage in 2021.[19]

The Toyota Production System (TPS) that enables building high-quality products with the lowest possible cost and on-time delivery is the backbone of Toyota's success if you talk to anyone outside Toyota. Although that performance of TPS is true, the TPS itself is not a secret, and it's widely available for all vehicle manufacturers as well as other industries like hospitals, airports, or even restaurants. But the secret sauce behind Toyota's success is that they do the small things well. They stay alert about all uncertainties. With that level of attention reaching down to even the lowest-rank employee, everyone in the organization has the power to make decisions to create an organization in which they feel pride in what they do.

While Toyota is able to get the best out of Fredrick Taylor's scientific management with TPS, it also gets the best out of people by remaining alert about the unknowns and getting the small things right. Toyota also faced multiple crises like any other large company, but it did not divert Toyota's path and did not destroy the organization.[20]

At Toyota, when a defect is detected, the lowest-level operator can stop the production line to prevent a bad-quality part from escaping the production line. That's how alert every person is at every level. Other companies can copy the mechanical aspects here, but the human part of the management system is critical and harder to copy.

## COMPLEX ADAPTIVE SYSTEMS

By now, if you think that numerous factors and interrelations lead to behaviors that are hard to predict, you get the idea. You are right. It is difficult, if not impossible, to predict these interrelations and the behaviors; hence, the outcome is uncertain in complexity paradigm. Systems scientists call these types of systems complex adaptive systems (CAS).

In the knowledge era, we cannot treat people, or the systems built around people, like machines. We must instead treat people and organizations like organisms. Understanding that concept will give leaders today the tools they need to lead organizations well in the knowledge era.

It's a leader's job to create the system and culture—to get things done and done well. If something fails, fix it. But if many things fail, it's a leadership problem.

For example, if a customer, in this case an organization, beats up a supplier by continually asking for price reductions, and a business-to-business supplier gives in and cuts the price, the supplier will go bankrupt. If another supplier says, "No, we won't cut the price because we can't afford it," that supplier will say, "We won't do business with you." Then, the customer will be stuck with a low-quality, financially unstable supply base, which will lead to supply chain crises and poor quality.

Isn't leadership the root cause of the problem?

This kind of adversarial relationship causes all kinds of problems up and down the supply chain—and they all start when leaders do not create a culture of respect around the role of each person or entity involved in the process.

The balance is something that leaders juggle every day. For leaders to embrace complexity, they must be willing to learn from suppliers and customers alike.

If there are problems with either side, the blame falls squarely on leadership.

## EVERYDAY SCENARIOS

When a new leader is hired, the hiring manager celebrates the success of getting a top gun to fill the role. The new leader then starts the job, and the organization interacts, learns, adapts, and evolves depending on how the new leader behaves. The organization changes under the new leader.

If the new leader isn't a good one—perhaps he failed to deliver in the past and never learned from his mistakes—the organization will know. Maybe the hiring manager didn't see the red flags, but the people with whom the leader has to interact on a daily basis will change in negative ways.

Often the people within the organization go into "wait and see mode." Maybe the new leader will figure things out and change course. Other times, good people quit, become defensive, lose efficiency, become unmotivated, and lose respect for the big boss who hired the bad leader.

When such disapproval happens, the leader obviously can't get things done or deliver on his commitments. The organization is not with him—and he can't force it to be.

In fact, I knew a leader who had an experience just like that. He had a bad history but nevertheless was appointed to lead the team. In his mid-40s, he was known as Michael. He had a bad reputation both personally and professionally, with continual compliance issues, and had been fired multiple times.

Michael changed his name to a new name—let's call him Tom—and with it, a new job.

He went through the interviews and background checks with none of those concerns cropping up. Six months later, Tom's boss got a bad feeling. Some female colleagues expressed discomfort to even sit next to Tom, and his team came to know about his past and the true Michael.

The team distanced themselves from him. Then, Tom's boss found out the truth about Michael. He sat down with Tom and had a tough conversation, basically saying there were only two options moving forward: Tom could either go home that day, or there would be zero tolerance moving forward.

Since then, Tom has been very open about his past. His actions backed up his desire to change, and his own organization changed for the better. In this successful case, Tom changed to be better. What if he could not or would not change? Then he needed to be removed from the organization to protect the organization.

We'll talk more about tough-love interactions for knowing and leading people like Michael and Tom in part IV of the book.

Hiring a bad leader doesn't have to destroy an organization. If leaders understand the complexity, continually engage on these critical organizational matters, and are willing to have tough interactions, and the behavior does change, organizations can thrive despite the first mistake. Organizations are complex adaptive systems, and the complexity can work in a leader's favor too. You cannot stop organizations from changing. But you can make the change work for you rather than against you to get things done. That's the art of complexity leadership.

## BOEING: THE 737 MAX COMPLEXITY

At this stage, it's clear that organizations are complex, and they continue to evolve. When leaders are under pressure to deliver results, it is all too possible for them to spend all their time on driving results rather than on embracing complexity by understanding where the organization is evolving.

Let's look at an example that showcases the importance of leaders embracing complexity.

In December 2013, Dennis Muilenburg was named the president of Boeing, the American aircraft manufacturer. He joined Boeing in 1985 as an intern, going through engineering and program management, and worked his way up to the head of Boeing Defense, Space & Security (BDS) before heading to lead the Boeing Company as its president.[21]

With the promise to increase profit margins from about 9% to the "mid-teens,"[22] Muilenburg deployed a massive headcount reduction program, as he had done successfully in the Boeing defense business. He continued these headcount reduction efforts even after he became the CEO in 2015, and despite the increasing sales, headcount was reduced by 13%. Wall Street loved Muilenburg.

He appeared in *Bloomberg Markets* magazine in an article titled "Up, Way UP," and he was named *Aviation Week*'s person of the year. Highly motivated by improved margins and cash flow with cost cuttings, Boeing also started an insourcing program to build aircraft parts.[23]

In a reversal of a previously established outsourcing strategy, Boeing set up an in-house unit called Boeing Avionics in 2017. The unit was dedicated to the development and production of avionics and electronics systems.

In a company memo to employees, Muilenburg said, "We can further drive cost down and value up for our customers," the same strategy used by previous leaders for outsourcing the same parts.[24]

Insourcing is not a bad strategy. But you don't do that without understanding the real costs and building the real technical know-how associated with it, which either takes years to build or requires a strategic acquisition. Think of it this way: If you run a restaurant, you probably don't produce your own milk too. It's expensive and requires a different set of knowledge. At a restaurant, you'd better be cooking food and serving it—not growing vegetables, raising livestock, and more—if you want to have a business that can function on a larger scale. If full vertical integration is the strategy, it needs time and careful execution to make it happen.

Innovation and safety are more critical to compete in the airline industry. With continual cost reductions, it is impossible to keep up. Innovation then becomes a target for many leaders when they look at ways to cut costs to

## WHAT IS COMPLEXITY AND WHY DO YOU NEED TO CARE

deliver short-term profits. Let's see what happened at Boeing despite its leader's promises and plans to improve margins and deliver superior performance.

Boeing's biggest rival, European aircraft manufacturer Airbus, launched the A320neo aircraft ahead of Boeing's competitive product offering, the 737 MAX. Boeing rushed the production ramp-up of the 737 MAX to compete with the A320neo in order to secure orders.

On October 29, 2018, the Boeing 737 MAX aircraft, operated by Lion Air Flight 610, crashed into the Java Sea near the Bornean islands of Indonesia 13 minutes after takeoff, killing all 189 passengers and crew.

On March 10, 2019, the Boeing 737 MAX aircraft operated by Ethiopian Airlines Flight 302 crashed near the town of Bishoftu in Ethiopia six minutes after takeoff, killing all 157 people aboard.

The Chinese government was the first to ground all Boeing 737 MAX aircraft, and all other countries followed suit.

Investigations revealed that the Boeing 737 MAX suffered a recurring failure in the Maneuvering Characteristics Augmentation System (MCAS).[25] The company did not inform pilots or include a description of it in the flight manuals, leaving the pilots unaware of the MCAS.[26]

If it had been included in the flight manual, Boeing would not have received a Federal Aviation Administration (FAA) type certification, meaning delays and higher costs to get regulatory approvals to fly the plane.[27]

The MCAS is activated when there is a risk of stall, keeping the nose downward to prevent an undesirable angle of attack. If MCAS is activated, pushing the nose downward, it is hard for pilots to keep altitude. So, activating MCAS at lower heights is dangerous.

The general public and the regulators around the world wondered why MCAS got activated at lower heights in these two flights.

Investigations revealed that Boeing designed MCAS with a single sensor. If that sensor gives wrong information, there is no second sensor to verify the information, and MCAS acts on the only input. To have such an important product created without some kind of redundancy is madness. Whether in an aircraft or sensitive medical device, products that need to function properly to keep people alive need to be built with redundancies. Those are the things you don't take chances with. For aircraft engineering to have designed such a critical product without a redundancy seems obviously dumb, ignorant, or purposely done to reduce costs.

By going to such lengths to reduce costs, Muilenburg created a culture that led to poor quality. It's not a leap to believe the culture encouraged engineers to take chances on their designs and is why corners were cut in design.

Along with the accidents, Muilenburg's lack of engagement, personal connectivity, interactions with stakeholders, prioritizations, and behaviors were heavily criticized. On December 23, 2019, Muilenburg lost his job as the CEO.[28]

We can assume that Muilenburg did not know those cost reductions would create such a big failure. He did not know launching the 737 MAX with single-sensor MCAS would result in planes crashing. He did not plan for the company to lose billions of dollars in penalties, technical fixing, legal fees, and compensations, as well as unaccounted reputation losses. But that all happened.

Why?

The headcount reductions that worked in Boeing's defense business did not work when applied to the whole company. Some were concerned about breaking the business despite the fact it looked good on short-term financials. Although cost reductions are good and often required to stay competitive, at what point will those actions break a business? For instance, consider the following issues at Boeing:

> Was it smart for Boeing to launch the 737 MAX in the expedited ramp-up schedule to compete with the Airbus A320neo despite the 13% headcount reductions?
>
> Why was MCAS designed with one sensor without redundancy?
>
> Why weren't the pilots trained on the new system?
>
> Why wasn't MCAS mentioned in the flight manual?

Why was cost-reduction pressure so deep?

Why wasn't Muilenburg as engaged as expected during crisis management?

Why did his interactions with government agencies, media, and employees miss the mark so badly?

Did Muilenburg become another person chasing revenue and profits and transform his organization that way?

Those questions underline the complexity. What worked before does not work every time. There is a limit with cost reductions, and at some point, those cuts cost more than they are worth. It's possible to transform an organization's culture beyond repair. Usually, that manifests itself externally by damaging the company's reputation beyond repair.

It doesn't matter that Muilenburg did not design the MCAS. The engineers did. Interconnectivity is one of the biggest elements of complex systems. Outcomes emerge from the actions taken by people at all levels of an organization—not just the top. But the top always influences those actions and, therefore, is accountable for the outcome.

Leaders must recognize that they are responsible for the whole organization and embrace complexity.

## ON BECOMING A COMPLEXITY LEADER

Dave Snowden, who worked for IBM Global Services, came up with a conceptual framework called the Cynefin model to help leaders in making decisions.[29]

According to the Cynefin model, when there is high order and the structure is clear, problems can be either small or large.

Small, obvious, or clear problems are easy to fix, and they can be solved through the process of sense, categorize, and respond. Policies and standard operating procedures will take care of these types of problems.

For example, say you go home and realize you're out of milk for your morning cereal. That's a small problem with an easy fix. It might be annoying after a long day at work, but you can simply go to the grocery store and buy more.

Large or complicated problems require expertise and analysis. Still, these problems also can be solved by the process of sense, analyze, and respond. Let's say on the way to the grocery store to get milk, you get into a car accident. The mangled vehicle is a complicated problem. You don't have the expertise to fix it yourself, but you can take your car to a mechanic who can analyze what's wrong with the car and fix it.

Then there are chaotic problems. A problem is chaotic when the problem is new and the order has not been established. Boeing 737 MAX crashes were a chaotic problem. Or if there's a fire in your kitchen, that is a chaotic problem. When COVID-19 first appeared in Wuhan, China, that also was a chaotic problem. When new problems happen, you quickly act to put out the fire or stop the bleeding. Then you establish order. So, the chaotic problems can be solved by the process of act, sense, and respond.

Last, there are complex problems. With these problems, it is hard to find out what is causing what outcome. There are unknown unknowns. In most organizations, leaders deal most often with complex problems. Because the outcome is uncertain, organizations continue to change and evolve. Leaders are expected to continue to get engaged, master complexity, then probe, sense, and respond to the problem.

Going back to George Floyd's case, it was a simple problem for the store clerk to call the police when he suspected a counterfeit bill. For the police to arrest Floyd and let judges and the legal system deal with it would have been a complicated problem, complete with expert analysis to find out if Floyd was wrong. Instead, the actions from the police officer created a chaotic situation. Fellow police officers failed to intervene when they witnessed their colleague taking drastic, unnecessarily cruel actions. A simple problem instantly became a complex problem, which evolved in different shapes and on a large scale, involving all parts of the country and demanding accountability and system-wide change for Floyd's death.

Some say complex problems are people problems. In a way, there is merit to that argument in a practical perspective. Organizations are complex because people interact, are interdependent, learn, adapt, and evolve to a better stage always. Most leaders will tell you they spend most of their time dealing with complex problems.

The people problems are the hardest problems leaders deal with. Leaders who understand this complexity don't delegate to others the hiring, integration, firing, conflict resolution, provision of accurate feedback, and behavior-improvement needs. Leaders spend more of their time on these people decisions and interactions than all else combined. Nothing is more important with consequences being longer lasting than the people decisions. Leaders must be comfortable handling those responsibilities. Once you embrace complexity, you will be comfortable tackling complexity and get your people decisions right.

There are standard operating procedures and experts to handle obvious and complicated problems, and frankly there are merits in industrial age leadership theories that work in solving these problems. Chaotic problems don't come up regularly unless the organization is completely broken, or you are really unlucky.

Successful leaders know how to tackle complexity. To do so, they must be comfortable with

- knowing complexity,
- thinking about complexity,
- seeing complexity,
- trusting complexity,
- feeling complexity,
- acting complexly, and
- being complex.

In short, leaders must embrace complexity. Once you embrace complexity, we can get to the rest of the hard work involved with being a complexity leader with the use of the SIILA model for tackling complexity when the outcome is uncertain.

Many books cover how to get others to do the kind of work you want them to do. In this book, we won't be talking about how to manage others. We will talk about how to manage yourself, as a leader. After all, if you cannot even manage yourself, there is no chance of managing others.

## SIILA MODEL WITH TOUGH-LOVE INTERACTIONS IN TACKLING COMPLEXITY

We love our children. Because we love them, we correct them and even punish them when they misbehave in order to raise better adults. This is a tough-love interaction.

Tough-love interaction is the foundation of the SIILA model in tackling complexity. Leaders, like anyone else, love themselves. But leaders are very tough on themselves in that they study hard, work hard, and sacrifice a lot, such as time, family, hobbies, sleep, or health. They also face tremendous political and performance pressures.

Tough love will not always make you and your people happy, but it will make you and your people successful and safe.

The SIILA model will make you practice these tough-love interactions with yourself in making you a complexity leader. The method starts with getting into the right mindset through systems thinking and internalization. It's then followed by tough-love interactions with all levels of the organization inside and outside. After these tough-love interactions with others, you learn and adapt.

By mastering the five steps of tough-love interactions in the SIILA model for tackling complexity when the outcome is uncertain in the knowledge era, leaders can get things done and deliver consistently time and time again.

## SIILA MODEL FOR TACKLING COMPLEXITY WHEN THE OUTCOME IS UNCERTAIN

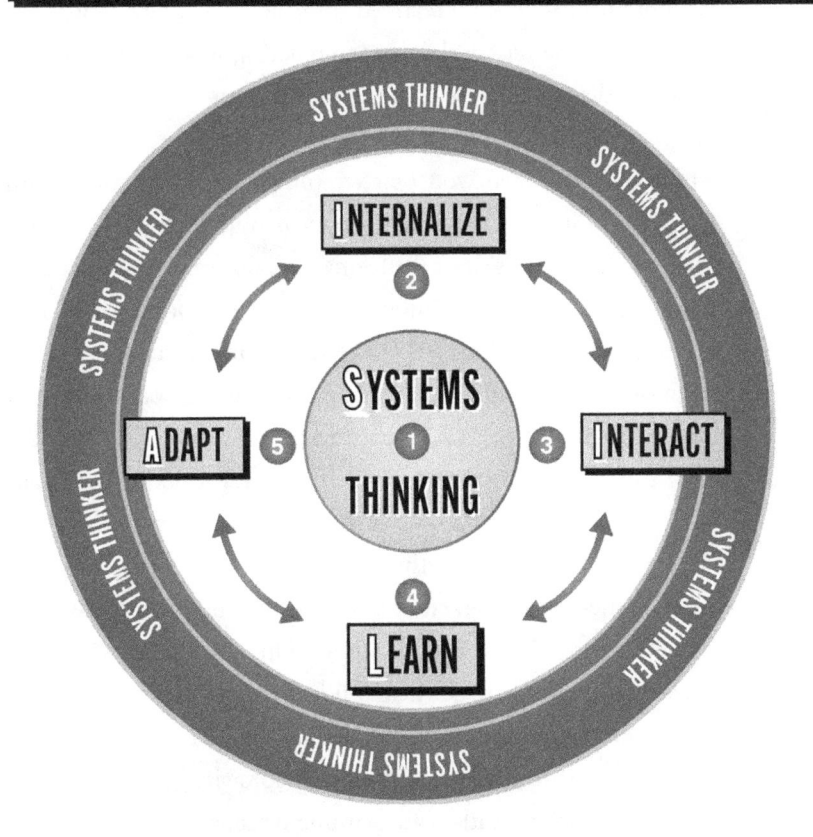

1. **Systems Thinking:** The whole is better than any one person, including the leader and any one aspect of the organization. When leaders master systems thinking, they understand how different parts are interconnected, meaning an organization will have the right mindset to create appropriate processes and structures that drive positive outcomes and avoid unintended negative outcomes. We'll talk more about this in part II.

2. **Internalize:** This step is the most important part of tough-love interactions with yourself. It calls for you to master yourself and understand your real motivations on becoming a leader. If you can internalize systems thinking and complexity, your personal values become unconsciously integrated into each and every action you take. This is the real deal. There's no acting here. Part III of the book will discuss how to align the motivations for leadership and master yourself.

3. **Interact:** In this step, you practice tough-love interactions with the organization. In the organization, people interact with each other inside and outside of the formal and informal organizational structures. Leaders must interact at all levels, too, if they want to know what they don't know. Leaders won't learn what's really going on in the organization just by being in the boardroom and talking to only their direct reports. In part IV, we'll talk about the art of tough-love interactions, which includes speaking with candor to get the best out of the organization without breaking the organizational order to get things done.

4. **Learn:** When you interact, you are part of the complex system. You will learn what you don't know. This knowledge gives you power. The power comes when you have the knowledge. To have knowledge, you must know the details. In part V of the book, we will discuss how leaders can identify knowledge gaps, learn to manage themselves, and create learning organizations.

5. **Adapt:** Organizations continue to adapt and evolve, for better or worse. When you master systems thinking and internalize complexity leadership, through tough-love interactions, you discover the knowledge gap, you learn how to fix it, and then you adapt. Just like a complex system, you change yourself as a leader and thus transform the organization. We'll talk more about this in part VI of the book.

This process isn't a one-time process. As a leader, you must be continually probing and engaging, making the process continue within the systems thinking framework as shown in the SIILA model diagram. When you make SIILA a never-ending loop, SIILA becomes a habit, and you will tackle complexity and get things done in work and life continually.

# PART I REVIEW

In part I, we discussed the complexity that leaders must tackle today to get things done. Here are the key takeaways:

- Living things, including people, organizations, societies, and markets are complex. They continue to evolve, so the outcomes of the decisions are uncertain, and unless leaders tackle complexity, they cannot get things done and deliver performance.
- Leaders must spend more of their time on people decisions and interactions than all else combined because nothing is more important or has longer-lasting consequences than people decisions.
- In the five steps of systems thinking, internalize, interact, learn, and adapt, the SIILA model provides a step-by-step approach for tackling complexity and getting things done when the outcome is uncertain.

Next, we will discuss systems thinking as the foundation for tackling complexity.

# PART II

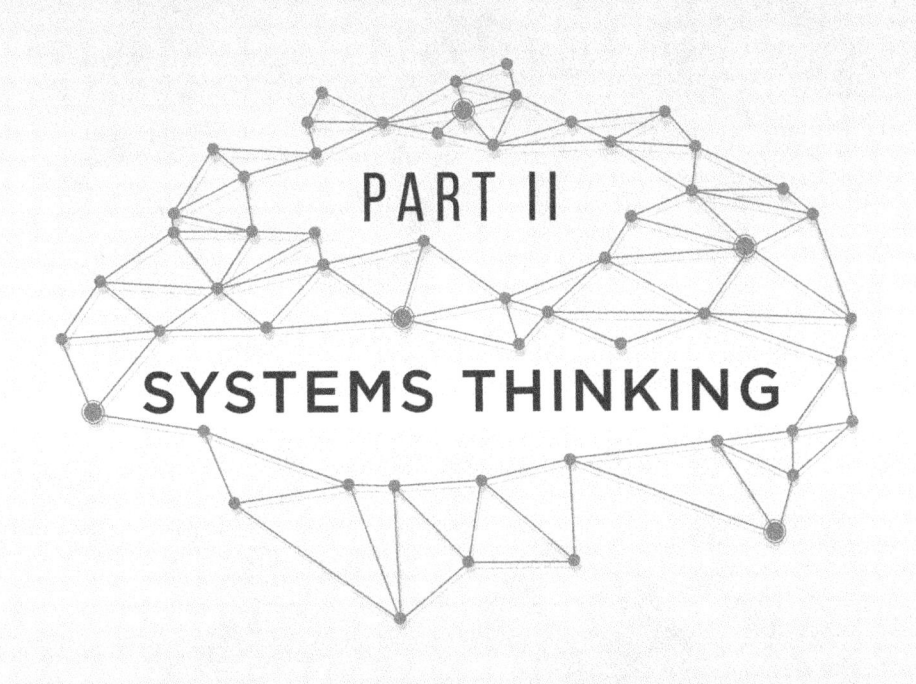

# SYSTEMS THINKING

# CHAPTER 3

# HOW THE BOARDROOM AND SHOP FLOOR ARE CONNECTED

To tackle complexity, it's critical for leaders today to understand how everything is interconnected in the space where people, machines, materials, and movements take place.

James Lovelock, an English scientist known for his work as an environmentalist and futurist, devised the Gaia hypothesis. This hypothesis suggests that the earth is a complex system in which living organisms interact with their inorganic surroundings in a sort of mutually beneficial way to maintain the kind of climate and biochemical conditions necessary to live on Earth.[30]

Said another way, it's a theory that the things that create livable conditions on Earth, such as oxygen levels, water, climate, and acidity, are maintained as a result of the automatic, unconscious feedback process that happens within the interactions between living organisms and their inorganic surroundings.

That hypothesis can be extended to business too. Everything is interconnected.

How can a business leader grow their business, bring in more profit, or have massive success if they don't understand the value of everything else in the proverbial ecosystem?

For long-term economic success, business leaders must recognize that all of these aspects are interdependent. You can't remove economic success, environmental stewardship, healthy work culture, or societal influence from the equation. They all are connected.

That's why investors today, beyond pure financial metrics, look at other criteria such as environmental, social, and governance (ESG) to evaluate the long-term value of an investment. It's a set of standards many investors use to screen potential investments and evaluate a company's standings. As for the environmental aspect, the index evaluates how a company functions as a steward of nature. Does it dump toxic waste into local villages' drinking water? Or does it plant trees to help offset carbon emissions? Socially, the index evaluates how it navigates relationships with employees, customers, suppliers, and the communities surrounding it. Do employees regularly sue the company because they feel they've been mistreated? Or do employees generally feel good about where they work and for whom? The governance aspect of the index speaks more directly to the company's leadership, examining executive pay, audits, internal controls, and shareholder rights.[31]

The tricky part is there is no single metric that is more important or more worthy of leaders' attention. They all are critical for the long-term viability of a modern company. Leaders who fail to understand how connected these factors are will struggle to get things done.

It's also critical for leaders to realize that the whole of an organization is more important than any one person or any one thing—including the leaders themselves. The leader will never get what they want done or achieve their goals unless everyone in the system also achieves their own goals. Everyone's good, life, freedom, and happiness are important. It's not just the leader who needs those things.

Here's another way to think about it.

Nearly 200 years ago, Victor Hugo said, "He who opens a school door, closes a prison."[32] The idea behind his insight is that education can save people from a life of crime. School can change people's behavior and show them an alternative path so they don't end up in prison.

The two are interconnected.

One study from UC Berkley that looked into the effect of education on crime found that "schooling significantly reduces criminal activity" for a number of complex reasons.[33]

That same study estimated that every 1% increase in high school completion rates in men ages 20–60 could save the U.S. $1.4 billion each year in reduced costs associated with crime.

It's safe to extrapolate that having access to the right education deeply influences people's mindsets. Education does more socially and economically to reduce crime than hiring more police officers and establishing more courts and prisons.

Make no mistake, there are highly educated people who are in prison too. Being educated doesn't mean you will follow the law. But it certainly gives you an advantage.

Why are we talking about this?

It's important to set the stage and remind ourselves of the interconnectivity of complex systems and all that is involved and at stake.

In systems science, one of the first things we learn is that the system you want to study is defined by the boundaries you make. This book is about getting things done within organizations—so, our boundaries aren't necessarily as broad as something like the Gaia system, but the general idea still applies.

In understanding that aspect of the complex adaptive system, let's take a deeper look at how organizations are interconnected.

## ORGANIZATIONAL INTERCONNECTIVITY

In your business, you typically run things according to your business plan. You arrange your employees, floor space, capital, and other resources as best you can to support your overall goal. There are all kinds of sophisticated computer models, finance departments, and systems that can help you do it—from capital budgeting, to floor space requirements, to pricing policies. These decisions are interconnected. For example, if you don't invest in capacity expansion, you don't grow your business.

That simplicity is the easy part of interconnectivity. Good leaders today must stay on top of those aspects, of course, but they can't afford to get too mechanical in the process or underestimate the complexity of getting things done, which is a game totally different from resource allocation.

Leaders typically have a great mission, vision, and strategy. That's why they are leaders. Leaders don't usually fail because they lack those important parts of their plan. Leaders fail in executing that strategy. Getting things done is the hardest part.

To get things done, leaders hire a team, integrate them in the organization, and then manage the operational process to get things done.

When things go wrong, you have to ask, "Where did the leader go wrong?"

- Did they not hire the right people?
- Did they not integrate them well?
- Did they not manage the operations well?

They are all interconnected, and it is the leader's responsibility to manage all three competencies of hiring, integration, and managing operations if getting things done is the focus.

Recall what we learned in chapter 2. People problems are the most difficult problems leaders will have to tackle in their organizations.

Don't delegate hiring, integration, and operations management. These decisions are interconnected. If you hire someone who isn't a fit, it's your

## HOW THE BOARDROOM AND SHOP FLOOR ARE CONNECTED

fault, not theirs. Your ownership and accountability are important because you did the hiring and the integration, and you managed the operation.

Let's take a real-life example.

I once had an IT director who saw turnover of more than 100% in his organization. Everyone in his team got replaced within a year. Every time someone left, I heard comments like the following:

"It was a wrong hire."
"He did not get integrated well into the team."
"That person is no good anyway, so I let him go."
"He cannot take the pressure of the work."

When people leave a company at that rate, performance suffers. The leader will not get things done or deliver the expected performance. The leader will go on to develop a bad reputation for his leadership, as it looks like no one wants to work for him.

So I asked the IT director, "Which part of your job do you not know how to do? The hiring, the integration, or the operations management?"

It took some time and several rounds of discussions for him to realize he was the problem. *He* wasn't taking accountability for hiring, integration, and managing operations. Despite high levels of turnover, he blamed someone else when things went wrong until I intervened.

Eventually, he understood the problem. He explained the realization was like a light switch that turned on in a dark room, and he started seeing things clearly. He changed his own behavior and became one of the best people leaders on the team. The attrition levels went down, performance improved significantly, and his people, peers, and leaders really enjoyed working with him and his team.

Deep involvement doesn't mean that good leadership looks like micromanagement. A well-running organization still has strong delegation and empowerment. But because these things are interconnected, the leader is ultimately responsible and accountable for getting things done.

So, how does a leader go about overseeing and understanding relationships within an organization?

You've seen, probably even developed, a traditional organization chart. They have lines that connect employees to their direct reports, dual reports, and metrics reports, and standard operating procedures are outlined regarding how they should operate within the organization. There are a lot of formal structures. They might look different depending on a leader's particular taste and strategy to get things done, but you get the idea.

Almost all activities toward value creation require cross-functional teams and interconnections. They are interdependent. Members from engineering, finance, sales, legal, supply chain, IT, etc., may have different direct lines of reporting, but they all come together for value creation and are interconnected and interdependent.

In reality though, an organization is much more complex. Many interactions take place in all directions. Some employees and those in management positions may attend the same church, or their children may go to the same school. Some people may be on the same recreational sports team or support the same sports team. Some employees may be involved in current or former romantic relationships, and more.

Their associations aren't inherently bad. It's definitely not something a leader can prevent. People within an organization interact—but more than that, they are interdependent, regardless of the organizational chart or standard operating procedure.

Although the leader of an organization simply cannot maintain control over those relationships, a leader can set the tone for the culture, values, and beliefs within that organization. Throughout the book, we will discuss how a leader can go about doing that by implementing the SIILA model. In doing so, a leader will establish the boundaries of the environment in a way that influences the quality of the interactions throughout the organization and, therefore, will influence the quality of the work that gets done.

Here's what the interconnections look like daily in the workplace, in both formal and informal settings.

## REAL ORGANIZATION CHART

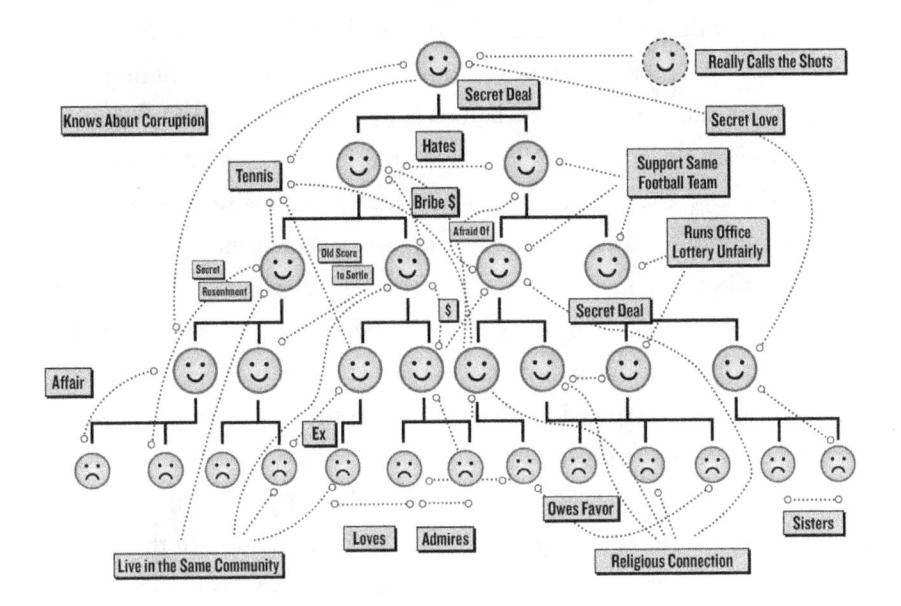

*[Organizational chart diagram showing smiley and frowny faces connected by various labeled relationships: Really Calls the Shots, Secret Deal, Secret Love, Knows About Corruption, Hates, Support Same Football Team, Tennis, Bribe $, Runs Office Lottery Unfairly, Secret Resentment, Old Score to Settle, Afraid Of, Secret Deal, Affair, $, Ex, Owes Favor, Sisters, Live in the Same Community, Loves, Admires, Religious Connection]*

## ORGANIZATIONAL DISCONNECT

During the production launch of the Saturn Ion car model in 2001, General Motors (GM) detected a faulty ignition switch. Technicians and engineers noticed the issue and proposed a correction to solve the problem with an estimated cost per car of less than $1.[34] Since the fix cost money, a decision was made not to change, and multiple other car models also launched with the same faulty switch.

In 2005, the first death caused by this faulty ignition switch was reported. A faulty ignition switch could cut off power and shut down the engine while the car was being driven. When accidents happen with the engine power cut off, the safety system can't deploy the airbags to protect the people in the car. GM, even after this incident, neither admitted nor fixed the issue. As a result, there were over 100 deaths and many other injuries reported due to the same technical issue.

In 2019, GM reached a $120 million settlement with vehicle owners who claimed their vehicles lost value due to the switch. It also shelled out more than $2.6 billion in penalties and other settlements, including $900 million to settle a criminal case launched by the U.S. Justice Department. The company also paid nearly $35 million in legal fees and expenses.[35]

In this case, the complex system that leaders dealt with included GM's own organization, customers, suppliers, government agencies, society, and media. It was probably not GM's CEO who told the engineer not to fix the faulty ignition switch. But that is how the message was understood within GM's organization. Investigations showed that even after 13 people died, someone at GM instructed engineers not to fix the design because it would cost $1 per car, an expense that was deemed too high.[36]

When one death happened, a message did come from society and customers to GM leaders through the channels of interactions. In these interactions, leaders had an opportunity to decide what actions to take. When GM leaders ignored these signals, interactions and interdependencies resulted in more deaths of customers, loss of company reputation, and billions of dollars spent in recalls and fines—and stakeholders to shareholders to customers lost value.

This example illustrates the power of interconnections and interdependencies in the complexity paradigm.

Here's another example that speaks to the complexity of the organizations and how CEOs see their interactions accelerate organizational productivity.

## MINGLING AROUND THE CORNERS

In the midst of the COVID-19 pandemic, many CEOs believed the workplace would see a significant change, especially in regard to employees returning to the office. Many believed staff would never fully return to the office. And as countries began to reopen, many employees continued to work remotely.

Recall Frederick Taylor's understanding of management, which basically believed managers could treat laborers as machines rather than as humans. This kind of industrial era management style would say interactions were bad, if they were allowed at all, which isn't much different from remote work.

But CEOs realized something. The culture and efficiency of the office were not the same when employees Zoomed in from home every day.

Humans are, after all, social animals. Coffee-corner talks, whispers during meetings, mingling around the corner, ride-sharing, and cafeteria chats matter. Humans work well when they are together. When employees share their personal lives, stories, and achievements, they are more motivated to achieve their goals together; hence, you see more productivity.[37]

## WHY IS THE LEADER HELD RESPONSIBLE FOR EVERYTHING?

Boeing's 737 MAX aircraft experienced crashes because the MCAS was designed with a single sensor and did not have the redundant sensor.

GM's Saturn Ion car ignition switch was faulty, causing fatal accidents because engineers did not fix the design prior to the launch.

Multiple project delays and technical issues with the Airbus A380 and Boeing 787 were mainly caused by poor supply chain decisions.

Many other problems are happening in organizations around the world, from missing financial commitments to quality issues, delivery issues, people issues, customer dissatisfaction, and fraud.

The leaders are held responsible for these things that happen even at lower levels of the organization. But where is the interconnection from leadership to these events that happen at the lowest level of the organization?

These events are only the tip of the iceberg.

Let's keep going with the iceberg metaphor. The density of ice is about 90% of the density of water; therefore, about 90% of an iceberg is underwater. A mere 10% is visible.[38]

You can think of the complexity in the organization in much the same way. The visible events—the things that go wrong—are only the tip of the iceberg. One would say you are unlucky or that you have a difficult job, but the really big problems—weak foundations and bad leadership—lie below the surface.

To be fair, the effect is the same for positive outcomes too. If you have beautiful, positive outcomes, some might say you are lucky or you have an easy job—but the really hard work, the strong foundation, and good leadership are below the water.

According to the iceberg model of systems thinking, the root cause of major events cannot be understood unless you go below the surface. There you can see patterns, structures, and mindsets that are created by the organization's leadership.

Knowing that fact, leaders must be systems thinkers to be effective in today's knowledge era. They can't spend all or even most of their time creating or reviewing charts in the boardroom.

Today's leaders must spend time creating and cultivating the right culture and values, which eventually drive the results.

## EASIER SAID THAN DONE

Every single person employed by an organization comes from a different background with their own experiences and their own value systems. To get everyone aligned with one value system is hard. But to get the ball rolling, leaders must serve as role models—and they do, whether they realize it or not.

The leader can create the organization the way they want it to be, the same way you create your own shadow. Stop blaming others when things go wrong. Leaders are accountable for everything that happens in the organization—good or bad. It's like when your children are misbehaving: You as a parent may have done something wrong. If leaders are not accountable, why should they get such titles, power, and compensation anyway?

That's why even if Dennis Muilenburg, the former Boeing CEO, did not personally direct the particular engineer to design the MCAS with one sensor, a design flaw that resulted in two plane crashes, Muilenburg was still responsible and lost the job. As with any large company, there might have been multiple reviews and more than one approval processes, but the issue still passed through. System structure did not fix the problem because at all levels involved the mindset accepted these approaches. Mindsets are a result of the culture the leader creates. Therefore, the leader is responsible.

Every company has great culture initiatives and core-value statements. They are written all over meeting rooms, computer screen savers, mouse pads, and big displays at the entrances of offices. But an organization's real culture and values are displayed underneath the surface, especially when companies make decisions about whom they hire, promote, or fire, as they are such powerful decisions that they can make or break the organization depending on the signal the leader sends.

For example, if one division of a company fires a bad employee for valid reasons but another division attempts to block the firing or hire the employee to that division, what does that tell you about the company culture? It isn't unified.

I once had to dismiss someone who was performing poorly. On top of the individual's poor performance, other employees under this person were leaving the company, and I discovered this person allowed behavior from his team that went against the company values and culture. Managers sent warning letters, and he was given another chance with a different location and department. But the employee's performance and behavior did not improve. So, I had to fire the employee to protect the rest of the organization. Another division wanted to hire this person onto their team, but we said no.

They pushed back until we asked this question: How can a person be bad for one division, not living up to the organization's values and culture, and be good for another division in the same company? So, finally we let that person go.

If a leadership team isn't unified, both sides will lose respect for the organization. No amount of culture training can fix this mindset. So, each people move matters. Leaders are expected to get engaged and kill bad culture and promote good culture every single moment. If this problem is escalated to the CEO, the focus should not be on firing or transferring the employee. Instead, the question should be "What's wrong with the culture of the company that different senior leaders interpret values and culture differently?"

If senior leaders are not aligned on the culture and values of the company, how could they possibly get lower-level employees aligned in that way?

In this example, as a result of firing that employee, the culture and the values of the organization improved and eventually led to better results.

The point is that systems thinking serves as the key for leaders to thrive in complexity. If a leader is unable to go beyond this system thinking, complexity leadership is not possible.

Recall the SIILA model we discussed in the last chapter. With this model, systems thinking is the boundary to cross to enter complexity leadership. Unless you embrace systems thinking, you cannot be a complexity leader.

## LEADERSHIP RESPONSIBILITY MODEL

The diagram below illustrates the interconnectivity and interdependencies from leadership, mindset, systematic structures, and patterns, to the events. A leader's positive influence on the mindset of the organization will create systematic structures to deliver patterns that eventually create positive outcomes.

Similarly, if the leader's behavior is leading to an undesirable mindset, then system structures will create bad patterns that lead to bad events or results.

# LEADERSHIP RESPONSIBILITY MODEL

## WHY LEADERS ARE RESPONSIBLE FOR EVERYTHING

**EVENT**
What is happening

WHAT YOU SEE IS 10%

WATERLINE

**PATTERNS**
What are the trends or patterns happening over time that create events

WHAT YOU DON'T SEE IS 90%

**SYSTEMATIC STRUCTURES**
What are the systematic structures that create patterns: organization charts, policies, standard operating procedures and power structure

**ORGANIZATIONAL MINDSET**
What is the mindset that creates systematic structures: morals, values, attitudes, behaviors, and culture

**LEADERSHIP**
What is the leadership behavior that creates organizational mindsets

⇧

**ULTIMATE RESPONSIBILITY**

If a leader is, for example, solely focused on costs, all his energy goes into driving costs lower. That emphasis creates a mindset of cost reduction. So, executives at the organization come to believe the only way for them to survive and keep their jobs is to carry out cost reduction. The mindset then cascades down the organization.

Maybe some leaders even create a system to reward those who make the deepest cuts in travel costs, bills of materials, new designs, headcounts, etc. That system may work for the singular goal of cost reduction—but it makes things harder, leading to bigger problems in the future, and ultimately organizations and leaders themselves fail.

Let's say we have a situation in which a company isn't meeting the budget, so it has to do cost cutting. The CFO says there's a hiring freeze and a travel freeze. But that CFO might be sitting 10,000 miles away from the employees and managers on the ground. How much does the CFO really know about the operation?

All of a sudden, controllers in the CFO's office publish a new travel-approval policy. Someone 15 levels up the chain needs to approve the purchase of a $10 train ticket for a quality engineer to go meet with a customer to resolve a field-quality problem. If general managers on the ground can't make that call, why have them in the job? Get a monkey or something!

What if the newly created processes mean a field-quality issue blows up bigger because a qualified engineer now can't travel?

What if a product design isn't made with appropriate safety precautions and fail-safe measures because redundancies weren't in the budget?

What if cost prevents engineers from bring up proposals to fix quality and safety issues?

Let's go back to the GM faulty ignition switch and Boeing 737 MAX's poor MCAS design with no redundant sensors. In both cases, those shortcuts reduced immediate costs. But the end result was losing billions of dollars, losing consumer confidence, and losing hundreds of lives.

It's fair to ask if company leadership created mindsets of cost reductions at any cost and hence created systematic processes and structures that way. In these cases, the patterns may have been cost reductions without considering the risks or lack of ability to balance the risk.

Remember there is no single metric more important or more worthy of leaders' attention than any other. For the long-term viability of the company, they all are critical. Short-term operational performance is critical to ensure the company survives until the investments for the long term begin producing returns. Financial performance is critical, but equally important is the ESG performance to ensure long-term sustainability.

Depending on the priorities at times, leaders might have to focus more on certain areas, but they must avoid creating a mindset that encourages others to ignore everything else and focus on one factor. The same thing will happen if a leader focuses too much on long-term innovations and not enough on what the company needs on a day-to-day basis.

Leaders who continue to interact with all levels of the organization, learn, and adapt will manage these risks much better than others who don't.

Leaders' behavior changes an organization, sometimes for the better and sometimes for the worse. Either way, organizations emerge based on leaders' behavior. In the next chapter, we'll talk about this emergence.

# CHAPTER 4

# YOUR ORGANIZATION HAS A MIND AND LIFE OF ITS OWN

Every single leader would say they are leading a transformation right now. These transformations could be anything from changing their operational footprint, organizational structure, or turnaround to redefining products, entering a new market, fixing broken operations, starting a digital transformation, launching a cultural transformation, and more.

As they should, leaders, by definition, challenge the status quo and lead transformations to make things better. Leaders spend a lot of time and money to do so. They hire experts, create transformation teams, and review and approve proposals based on the great benefits their company will achieve after the transformation.

For example, a leader may notice they can consolidate three regional business units into one global business unit so they don't have to reinvent the wheel in each region, all the while increasing visibility, eliminating support functions and overhead, and increasing profit by 5%. The leader gets excited, and consultants and transformation teams may even show how it was done and worked in other places.

But what if 12 months later the outcome is that local teams find it extremely difficult to convince global leaders about local customer needs, so customers get frustrated with the lack of local flexibility? The company could lose customers, and the business could become unprofitable. By that time, transformation teams may have already declared victory and moved on to the next project. The leader and the remaining stakeholders are stuck with the problem.

What is happening here?

There is no right or wrong answer when it comes to organizational design. But it depends on how leaders manage transformations and get things done. Although the leader wanted to transform the company from state A to state B, the company ended up in state C.

You have seen this outcome happen when a company hires a bad leader, as discussed in part I. Although the hiring manager celebrated hiring a top gun who could fix all problems, in the end, the business became worse than before.

So, why did this happen?

The transformation team may have done everything right, mechanically. But we're talking about a deeper process here.

The term *emergence* best explains this result and reflects the natural behavior of these kinds of transformations.

## EMERGENCE

At first, the term *emergence* might sound like the next blockbuster alien movie, unless you are a complexity scientist. But it actually describes an essential part of systems thinking.

Emergence describes how collective behaviors develop from the surrounding environment and transform into a different state. It applies to everything from how the universe came together, to how ants are able to work together to create colonies without advanced brains, to how social movements develop, and even how businesses come together.

It's the idea that small, individual parts come together, interacting and self-organizing to create whole new patterns. We accepted that organizations are complex adaptive systems (CAS), and emergence is a primary property of CAS.

To better understand the concept of emergence, let's look at the term *emerging adulthood*, initially defined by Jeffrey Jensen Arnett.[39] This term describes the development of teenagers into young adults, from ages 18 to 29. This age is about the time when teenagers leave home, find love, complete their education, find jobs, get married, start a career, start a family, identify their own personalities and beliefs, and more.

We know that everyone gets older, but not all become responsible, full-fledged adults who are independent and good citizens. Some will emerge to be positive (good), and some will emerge to be negative (bad).

It is the same for organizations. But the time frame for organizational emergence is typically much shorter than emerging adulthood.

We see this effect playing out in real time, every day in business. Organizations can transform in a positive way to makes things better. Organizations can also transform in negative ways to make things worse.

With the Boeing example, Dennis Muilenburg did massive cost reductions with good intentions and expected the transformation would be reduced costs, better profits, and a higher share price. In reality, this direction led employees to focus more on cost reduction and less on safety, resulting in a crisis.

People, organizations, society, and markets are complex. We can be sure of one thing for all of them: they will change naturally.

Here's a micro example: One of my friends was complaining to me recently about his wife. He got married to a very nice lady. She grew up in the countryside and enjoyed her simple life. When they got married, he brought her to Shanghai where she went to university and got an MBA. She went to work at a bank, and because she was very good at her job, she got promoted. Now, she's focused on her career.

My friend told me he was upset that she changed. She was no longer the country girl he married. She is an office lady now.

"What did you expect?" I asked him. "You took this smart lady and put her in a big city. What did you expect to happen? It's ridiculous to think she wouldn't change. Your problem is you didn't change."

People are complex. When they change, it is very natural. We see this complexity more frequently in the knowledge era, especially with skyrocketing divorce rates. People change while others may not be able to accept or keep up with the change.

We see this in the workplace too. Long-term employment is a thing of the past. Promotions and high pay do not guarantee you will keep good people. You have to continually engage with employees and allow them to change and even embrace them as they do. You must continue to offer hope and inspire them to work for you.

The emergence or the natural transformation happens from the individual level to the organizational level to the global economy. Here's a big picture example:

The United States emerged as a superpower after World War II, but that wasn't necessarily the country's intention. Up until that point, the United States was content letting Great Britain manage that responsibility.

By the end of the war, the United States was on a strong economic footing, as it had become the world's leading manufacturer, and it didn't want to give up its newly found position. So, the country took an active role in rebuilding cities torn apart by war. This effort helped the superpower create new markets to export goods, bolstering its economic influence.[40]

You can also look at how China emerged as a global economic power. In 1979, Deng Xiaoping rolled out his Open Door policy, allowing China to test the waters of the free market system. China's growth increased exponentially after joining the World Trade Organization in 1999. Today, China is the largest market for many industries, and many global companies see their fastest growth and largest share of revenue and profits coming from China. China's economy is projected to overtake the United States to become the world's largest economy within the decade.[41]

So, what does this emergence look like on a business level? How can a leader influence his own organizational emergence?

## MAKING THE GRASS GREENER ON YOUR SIDE

Let's take a look at how Ken Melrose transformed Toro, the landscaping equipment company. He transformed the company mindset, and a new organization emerged to design safer products, improved customer experiences, and reduced costs. That work eventually improved profits.

But before that, for years when customers reported getting injuries from Toro's lawn mowers, the company would go to court and battle it out. Toro was so proud of their products that it became arrogant when customers complained about the product quality.

For years, Toro defended itself vigorously. If someone suggested the lawn mower was at fault or had caused an accident, Toro fought with a lawsuit.

During the 1980s, the company faced major financial trouble. It was then that it named Melrose as CEO.

Melrose encouraged employees at all levels to speak up when something seemed wrong, and some in the company started to wonder if they should approach the injuries differently.

They suggested that instead of immediately beginning with court proceedings, someone from the company should sit down with the customer and show compassion. Toro put a process in place to dispatch a team, which included engineers and paralegals, to visit the injured customer.

The paralegal would sit down with the customer, express Toro's regret about the injury, and ask what happened. The paralegal would also explain that the customer was welcome to contact an attorney if they wanted to, but that Toro also wanted to do what it could to satisfy their concerns first.

The engineer came along to investigate the accident and see if there was a way to change the product to make it safer in the future. These investigations did ultimately lead to some changes in product design. One of the most notable changes was the safety shield that now hangs at the back of the mower. The shield prevents feet from sliding underneath and making contact with the sharp blade.

The team was also authorized to pay for the customer's medical expenses, lost work time, and more.

Let's look at the results of this change at Toro.

Toro retained more customers, and it actually cut costs. When Toro began its new method, termed *alternate dispute resolution*, costs fell 75% compared to the old approach. The average settlement cases fell to 53% of what they had been before.[42]

Melrose wasn't the one who came up with the idea that led to the cost reductions. But he did create an environment in which others felt comfortable sharing their ideas and speaking up.

In his book, *Making the Grass Greener on Your Side: A CEO's Journey to Leading by Serving*, Melrose wrote, "Everyone has the potential to contribute to achieving the goals of the company. If you unleash that potential, market leadership and financial success will be natural by-products."

Melrose went on to lead the company for nearly 25 years.

One person cannot achieve company goals alone. A leader's job is to unleash potential in their employees. So, the practical process of "getting things done" is about transforming the organization so that it emerges in a way that fosters everyone's true potential.

Melrose realized that the emergence of a company, whether it transforms into something good or bad, depends on the leader. He chose to be consciously engaged and embraced complexity. Because of his attention, his team performed well and did what they needed to do, even though he didn't tell them they had to do it.

So, how do we make sure we create a positive emergence? And how do we avoid a negative emergence? How do leaders embrace this emergence property of an organization and make it work for the leader to get things done instead of working against the leader?

## CREATING POSITIVE EMERGENCE

If I step outside my office and look around, I see around 50 people on the same floor. What do they do when I'm not around? I don't know. There are around 50 locations where our people work in manufacturing plants or offices that I can't and don't visit every day. I don't know what they do all day either. But I know work gets done. It is shown in monthly operational reviews, financial performance, and other performance metrics reviews. Reviewing metrics is exactly where leaders must spend *minimum* time.

Unfortunately, today leaders spend most time in reviewing charts and in the boardrooms, which is sad and probably the root cause of many leadership problems.

Instead, leaders should be continually engaged to influence the behavior of the organization.

In the simplest form, imagine the CEO of company A often meets with and tells its general managers: "My job is to support you. If you are successful, I have a chance of making myself successful."

In company B, the CEO tells its general managers: "You are stupid and dumb. You're getting free money while I do all the hard work."

Both CEOs are spending a lot of money and effort to transform the company to improve and deliver sustainable performance.

How will the CEOs' messages cascade down? How will the companies emerge?

Company B will emerge to be defensive. Good people will quit, and it will not achieve its goals. If the general managers of company B really are stupid and dumb, fire them and get good ones. But ultimately the leader owns the emergence of the organization. Leaders may not have time to visit all the people, but every interaction with an employee is an opportunity to send a message to all people.

Company A will become more aligned and motivated. Leaders will be open to sharing information, asking for help when needed, and taking ownership and being accountable. As a result, they will deliver on their performance expectations.

As you can see, creating positive emergence could be as simple as the statements you make. More critically, it can be about whom you hire, promote, and fire. All those areas lead to the emergence of the organization.

When leaders internalize that leadership is what creates the organizational mindset, they must consciously develop strong, positive workplace cultures. When people feel that they are doing meaningful work, they are personally and deeply connected with you and your leadership.

That connection will eventually lead to true organizational culture beyond posters and banners. People feel their value, and it will eventually lead to better products and services, improved quality and customer service, reduced attrition, and profitable growth.

## ELIMINATING NEGATIVE EMERGENCE

Leaders don't set out to fail or create a negative emergence that might take down a whole company. But it happens. The outcomes are uncertain, and leaders must always be on alert to sense if any negative emergence is starting to build up. That way they can stop it immediately before it gets out of control.

Let's take an example from workplace safety. We don't want our family members to lose a finger or arm on the job. Our employees are someone's child, relative, spouse, or parent. We cannot send them home disabled.

Most companies take workplace safety very seriously, and some use the loss workday (LWD) metric to measure workplace safety standards. If an employee cannot work due to an accident, it gets reported in an LWD report and generally circulated to senior management. But accidents still happen, and these are opportunities for leaders to learn more about the organization.

Are they really unpreventable accidents, or are they a result of bad leadership? That question is important to ask and verify. If these events are a result of bad leadership and you do nothing, something bigger and worse will happen later.

One of my plants reported an LWD case. A female operator crushed her left hand in a pressing machine, which caused multiple fractures. When I looked at the report, I noticed under the root cause eight items were listed.

When there is more than one root cause, leadership itself is the root cause. I investigated further.

The plant manager, under the pressure to deliver performance, pushed production supervisors hard to improve efficiency. These supervisors discovered that a safety device used to prevent access to the press while it was in operation was slowing things down. The operator had to open the safety shield, load the parts, close the shield, and run the press. If the safety shield was removed, it saved time, improved efficiency, reduced costs, and improved profitability.

My investigations also revealed the safety shields were removed from all 33 pressing machines in the plant.

There we had it. This one event led to me discovering a pattern of sacrificing worker safety. The plant manager created the mindset that improving profitability was more important than employee safety. Even if the plant manager did not say it directly, that was the mindset. That's why leadership is responsible for it.

I later visited the site with my human resources and operations directors to show our genuine care. I also shared the case study with everyone in the business and educated all plant employees on the importance of safety.

Just imagine how far this negative emergence—sacrificing safety to improve profitability—could have gone. It could have led to more accidents, poor product quality, more penalties, and higher costs. Thankfully, it didn't get to that point.

We speak about big disasters like the 737 MAX crashes, but when big disasters happen, it's too late to fix that negative emergence. There are always warning signals for leaders to sense negative emergences and react to them.

Some leaders will argue that they have no time to get into the details on every single issue. Yes, that is true, and everyone has a job to do. But leaders are ultimately responsible for getting things done and everything that happens in the organization. Leaders have to pick their battles. To a successful leader, there is nothing more important than fostering positive emergence. Pick your battles to create positive emergence and avoid negative emergence. That's tackling complexity.

# PART II REVIEW

In part II, we discussed systems thinking as it sets the foundation for tackling complexity. Here are the key takeaways:

- The whole of an organization is more important than any one person—including the leaders themselves—and therefore, for leaders to be successful and achieve their goals, everyone in the organization also must be successful in achieving their own goals.
- Leaders are held accountable for everything that happens in the organization, because leaders create the organizational mindsets that eventually lead to systematic structures, patterns, and events.
- Successful leaders manage themselves to be the role models, practice tough-love interactions, learn, and adapt to foster positive emergence to get things done as their top priority.

Next, in part III, we'll discuss the internalization part of the SIILA model and dive deeper into how to do it with more tough-love interactions.

# PART III
# INTERNALIZE

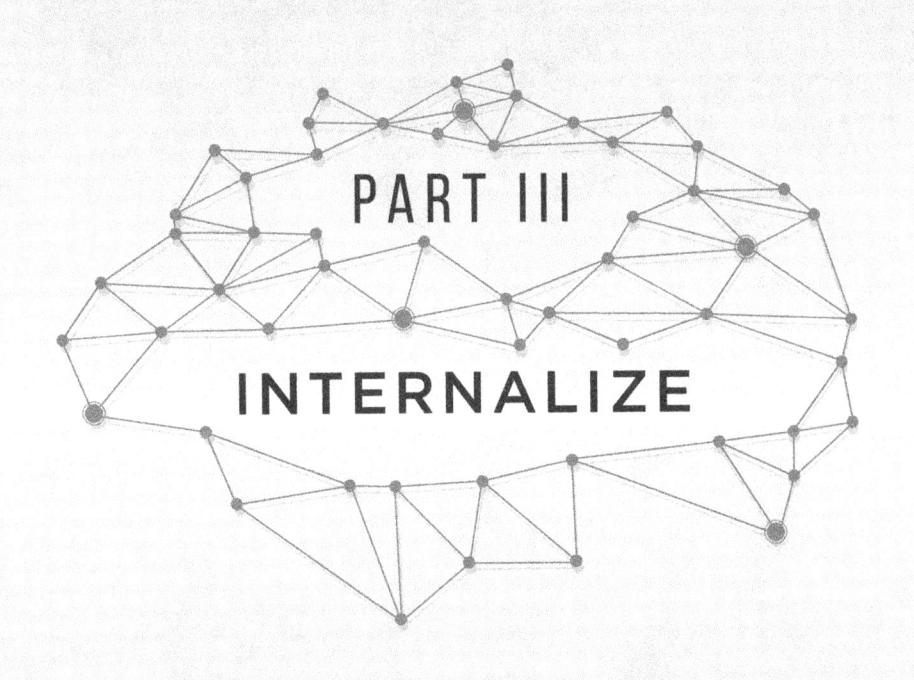

## CHAPTER 5

# WHY YOU NEED TO KNOW WHAT'S DRIVING YOU

In 2004, the president of Thunderbird School of Global Management, Angel Cabrera, created what he called a business oath. It's much like what the Hippocratic oath is to medical professionals. The oath takers use it to guide them through every decision in their career. I had the honor to take this oath in front of Professor Cabrera on the day I graduated with a master of global management from Thunderbird at Glendale, Arizona. The oath goes like this:

> *As a Thunderbird and a global citizen, I promise:*
> *I will strive to act with honesty and integrity,*
> *I will respect the rights and dignity of all people,*
> *I will strive to create sustainable prosperity worldwide,*
> *I will oppose all forms of corruption and exploitation, and*
> *I will take responsibility for my actions.*

*As I hold true to these principles, it is my hope that I may enjoy an honorable reputation and peace of conscience.*
*This pledge I make freely and upon my honor.*[43]

On graduation day, we received a nice card with this oath written inside it. I used to read it every day as a middle manager after the graduation. The words extolling the virtues of honesty, integrity, and respect, opposing corruption and exploitation, taking responsibility, and fostering sustainability were stuck in my head. Back then, I wondered why those concepts had to be taught. They seemed like the very obvious and correct things to do, and they seemed easy to put into practice. Didn't everyone work this way?

Today, I wonder how I could have been so naive. Leaders are either under pressure to deliver and do unethical things or are motivated by the wrong things.

Money, for example, can be a big motivator. It may tempt doctors to perform a $5,000 surgery on a patient rather than prescribing a $100 medicine if it means the doctor gets more money. A lawyer may extend litigation to get a bigger commission.

That's why the business oath—and internalizing what it says—is so important. Those temptations are everywhere.

And everyone from the shareholders to the general public knows it.

Building credibility and fostering an attitude of accountability have become a real challenge for business leaders, but both are critical. Practicing both is not about business skills; it's about the mindset and the motivations for the leadership that will help rebuild credibility and foster an attitude of accountability from the shareholders, to employees, to the general public.

## THE POWER OF THE MIND

I grew up in Sri Lanka where my parents sent me to Sunday school with my older siblings. When I was eight years old, unbeknownst to me, I sat for a national exam. I had no idea what I was doing. To me it was yet another day to play—but apparently, I did quite well. A few weeks later, my mother and I bumped into my Sunday school teacher. She said I passed the exam with honors.

I had no idea what honors meant, and it was news to me I'd taken an exam. A week later there was an award ceremony at the school, and I was given a fancy certificate and a book called *Dhammapada*. I still have the first page of that book memorized.

> Manopubbangama dhamma
> manosettha manomaya
> manasa ce padutthena
> bhasati va karoti va
> tato nam dukkhamanveti
> cakkamva vahato padam.

It is written in Pali, an ancient language of India derived from Sanskrit. It's the language of Buddhist scriptures. In Pali, mano means the mind, and it appears four times in the verse. The verse means this:

All mental phenomena have mind as their forerunner; they have mind as their chief; they are mind-made. If one speaks or acts with an evil mind, suffering follows him just as the wheel follows the hoofprint of the ox that draws the cart.

It essentially means the mind is so powerful, it is chief over everything. It's the mental phenomenon in which feeling, perception, and other mental formations cannot arise if the mind does not arise. It should be easy to understand when we think of how often we don't experience the taste of food while we're eating it, hear what someone says when they are talking, or see what's in front of us while we're looking at it. The mind is chief over everything.

The verse comes from what Buddha said more than 2,500 years ago to some monks who asked him why a fellow monk, named Cakkhupala, was blind.[44]

Buddha explained that in one of Cakkhupala's previous lives, he was a physician.

A blind woman came to him for help, hoping he could cure her. She was so desperate that she promised she and her children would become his slaves, forever indebted to him, if he could completely cure her.

He liked that deal, so he worked to cure her. She regained her sight, but fearing she and her children would live the rest of their lives enslaved, she lied to him. She told him her vision was getting worse.

The physician knew she was lying, so he took revenge. He gave her another ointment that made her totally blind. As a result of this evil deed, the physician lost his eyesight many times in his later existences.

I mention this story not to debate about whether rebirth is true or to spend much time thinking about the philosophy behind it. The point here is that the mind is powerful. Evil thoughts can lead to evil actions—and suffering follows, just like the hoofprint of the ox that draws the cart.

When I was eight years old, reading that verse and beginning to understand it, it scared me! I didn't even know how to spell the word *leader*, but I quickly understood that if you did bad things to others, bad things would happen to you.

Look around today. How many leaders end up in jail, lose jobs, destroy organizations, hurt people, damage society, and wreck the environment around them? Even if they don't get caught, they won't sleep well at night.

The mind is the key. That's why in the SIILA model of tackling complexity using tough-love interactions with yourself means internalizing the right motives. Once you internalize something, it becomes part of your nature. You will unconsciously repeat that behavior. There's no faking it here.

The great Chinese philosopher Lao Tzu said, "Conquering others is power. Conquering oneself is strength."[45]

The power of the mind is incredible. It can be used for good, or it can be used for evil, as the following examples show.

In 1945 when the Imperial Japanese Army surrendered, World War II officially ended. But one Japanese lieutenant, Hiroo Onoda, continued to fight until 1974—that's 29 years after the war ended. He was born into a family of warriors and studied unconventional military techniques in military school, including guerrilla warfare, sabotage, counterintelligence, and propaganda.

Hiroo Onoda was sent to the Philippines to fight against the American army. When the Japanese army lost the battle, Onoda and a few other soldiers fled into the jungles of Lubang Island in the Philippines. But they continued to fight.

Onoda and his men survived on a diet of stolen rice, coconuts, and meat from cattle slaughtered during farm raids in villages.

After the war ended, the U.S. Army used an airdrop of leaflets explaining that the war was over, but Onoda thought it was propaganda. Eventually, all of Onoda's men either left or died, until he was alone.

He continued to kill members of the Philippine military and innocent civilians for years. Not even the Japanese government could stop him. Together with family members of Onada, Japan, too, dropped leaflets and tried to get him to surrender. But he thought his family members had been captured by American forces and were under duress. So, he continued killing Philippine soldiers and innocent civilians. No one could take Onoda out of the jungle.

Another strong-minded Japanese explorer, Norio Suzuki, went to Lubang Island in the Philippines because it was one of his dreams to see Onoda. Suzuki met Onoda, but Onoda refused to come out, convinced he was still under orders and that the job was not yet finished. Finally, his seniors arrived and relieved him of his duty. Onoda complied. He was brought to Japan 29 years after the war ended.

However, Onoda was never comfortable with what Japan became, and he moved to Brazil, started a new family, and raised cattle. Eventually he returned to Japan and started a camp to train children be closer to nature.[46]

Hiroo Onoda shows us the power of the mind and the limits of how far values like loyalty, pride, determination, and commitment can take you with the power of the mind—for good or for ill. It can lead to dedication and courage, as well as stubbornness and delusion.

Mahatma Gandhi, the leader of India's independence movement, is the architect of nonviolent civil disobedience that influenced the world. His teachings inspired activists around the world, including Martin Luther King Jr., Nelson Mandela, and Malala Yousafzai.[47]

As a teenage girl, Malala spoke out publicly against the prohibition on the education of girls, survived an assassination attempt at the age of 15, and received the Nobel Prize.

It is the power of the mind, not money or military power, that helps such leaders achieve their missions.

## THE PSYCHOLOGICAL MIND OF BAD LEADERSHIP

Your title doesn't make you a good leader, no matter what position you hold.

Although there are no methods, formulas, or equations for leadership as Fredrick Taylor suggested, there are plenty of aspects that define good leadership and bad leadership.

As we discussed regarding the power of mind, we can conclude that bad leaders do bad things because they have a bad mindset.

Let's turn to psychology to gain an understanding about the mindset of bad leaders.

We don't often hear the term *dark triad* in our workplaces, but this is a popular term in psychology.

The dark triad refers to three personality traits that many psychologists consider the key to understanding why people commit crimes. The three personality traits in the dark triad are narcissism, Machiavellianism, and psychopathy. Below is a look at the dark triad from a leadership perspective.[48]

- **Narcissism:** The Greek myth of Narcissus says that a hunter fell in love with his own reflection in a pool of water and drowned, which sums up narcissism nicely. Leaders with narcissistic personality traits are selfish, boastful, arrogant, lack empathy, and don't take criticism.

- **Machiavellianism:** Italian diplomat Niccolò Machiavelli wrote a book called *The Prince* in 1513. It was interpreted by many to be an endorsement for leaders to commit immoral acts, such as deception or ruthless killing, in order to maintain their rule. Leaders with Machiavellianism show duplicity, manipulation, and self-interest, and lack emotion and morality.
- **Psychopathy:** Leaders with psychopathic personality traits lack empathy or remorse, exhibit antisocial behavior, and are manipulative and volatile.[49]

How can leaders avoid this dark triad?

If you're lucky, you were scared into always doing the right thing by children's stories that convinced you that bad things would follow you if you did bad things, just as the wheel follows the hoofprint of the ox that draws the cart. It may be childish, but it's worked for me so far.

If you didn't have the benefit of stories in your childhood scaring you straight, the threat of going to jail, paying massive fines, or losing your job might do it.

Fear really isn't the best motivator, but it certainly helps keep you on the right track until you've internalized what it means to do good.

Remember in the chapters on systems thinking, we talked about the need for the leader to realize the whole is more important than any one person in the system, including the leader himself? Leaders will never achieve their goals unless everyone in the system achieves their goals. So, it is important that leaders internalize that principle.

People will see through value statements, posters, big speeches, and town halls. They will be able to tell if you've internalized what it means to be a good leader. This is the knowledge era, and people are smart. We can't just act like good leaders—we must really be good leaders.

## WHY DO YOU WANT TO BE A LEADER?

This is a common interview question. If you Google it, you can find out what interview-preparation experts will say to guide you through this question. For example: I like the company vision and value system, opportunity aligns with my experience and next career goal, I have proven to be a good leader, or I hit the ceiling in my current role.

These prepared and well-rehearsed answers don't actually reveal much about what you have internalized about why you want to be a leader.

Some obvious perks might include being rich, powerful, and famous.

Most leaders earn more money. You can see their wealth by looking at their paycheck, the cars they drive, the types of holidays they go on, what house they live in, and what schools their kids attend.

Leaders also have a lot of social power. They get front-row seats, special welcomes, awards, first-class travel, and more.

Although those things are nice, they are exactly the wrong reasons to become leaders.

If the motivation is money and status, a leader will likely get frustrated when they have to do the hard work to keep the company moving forward. There are many well-paid jobs out there that offer the same perks of money and social status without getting into a leadership role if you really aren't cut out to be a leader.

Others are attracted to leadership roles because they think it will bring power or be more fun.

I've led organizations large and small, some with 10 employees, some with 30,000 or more people under me. Believe me, there is no real power in these leadership jobs. Instead, there is responsibility. Taking responsibility for every decision—good and bad—is very hard.

Just look at the before-and-after photos of any U.S. president as they take office and as they leave it. Nearly all emerge with gray hair and wrinkles that weren't there before. Sure, some of that is natural aging, but many experts point to the immense stress as a major factor.[50]

## WHY YOU NEED TO KNOW WHAT'S DRIVING YOU

When it comes to the prestige or social status heaped on leaders, many leaders out there would love to minimize that attention as much as possible.

It's much more fun to eat at a local restaurant in peace or to enjoy a homemade meal in comfortable pajamas than it is to eat a lavish meal while wearing a suit with 500 people watching and cameras following your every move.

It takes a lot of effort to endure those obligations and to conduct yourself well in public so often.

So, what is a good motivator? There are many good reasons to want to be a leader. They often come back to personal goals, people, or situational responsibility.

Some leaders may have a big dream or mission to make world greener, start space travel, create more jobs, invest in the next generation, and more.

Kindergarten teachers know ambition well. They enjoy helping people and seeing them grow. They help children grow beyond aspirations and love knowing that the children they taught are now doctors, professors, engineers, and presidents.

Good leaders are the same. The best leaders want to help people and see them grow. They know that by focusing on growing others, getting things done is much easier than most realize. It's the number one secret weapon in getting things done. To do it well, people must know you genuinely care about them and their success. Remember, there's no faking it here.

Good motivation can also stem from the desire to step up and meet a need. It might look like taking a leadership role to keep the family business alive or taking a senior job to ensure the organization is in good hands.

Regardless of the exact motivation, good leaders never do it simply to benefit themselves.

A big part of tackling complexity and getting things done through tough-love interactions when the outcome is uncertain is getting to the root of what motivates you as a leader.

Next, we'll dig deeper into internalization and the power of knowing yourself.

# CHAPTER 6

# POWER OF MASTERING YOURSELF

To tackle complexity, we must first start by tackling ourselves, which means understanding a few basic things about our own human nature.

We are in an inescapable relationship with ourselves. Like any other relationship in life, the relationship with self requires both love and respect.

Self-love gives us a reason to know ourselves, while self-respect requires us to embody our values and honor our commitments. To put those two things together means that we have to take every part of ourselves seriously.

The journey of finding yourself and discovering who you are, what you like, and what you dislike is a lifelong journey. It doesn't necessarily have a straight or smooth path (remember, humans are complex), but the journey well traveled will engage you deeply and force you to come face-to-face with your deepest fears, doubts, vulnerabilities, and insecurities. It also tests the limits of your values and morals.

Knowing yourself is the beginning of all wisdom. So, let's start.

We will first look at how Peter Drucker, the man recognized by many as the father of management, went on to know himself.

Before he died in 2005, Peter Drucker was celebrated by *BusinessWeek* magazine[51] as the man who invented management. Although many will associate his name with corporate management, his work fits the description well. Peter Drucker was driven to try to create what he called "a functioning society."

Drucker was a successful young investment banker in London in the mid-1930s. He was good at the work, but he did not see himself making much of a difference in the world. Drucker valued people more than he valued becoming rich.

He had to decide between his values and his work. He told himself that there was no point in becoming the richest man in the cemetery. Despite the continuing Depression, he quit his job. He had no money and no other job prospects, but he had made his decision.

Then he went on to become a consultant, academician, and author and is among the best-known and most influential thinkers on the matter of management theory and practice. He received over 25 honorary doctorates from different universities and multiple government recognitions, including the Presidential Medal of Freedom from U.S. President George W. Bush in 2002.[52]

## WHY DO YOU WANT TO KNOW YOURSELF?

Imagine a person who doesn't know who he is. This person laughs at what he thinks he is supposed to laugh at. He shows concern for what he thinks he is supposed to care about. He essentially conforms to the demands and expectations of others. He isn't motivated by the things he claims to be motivated by.

I've seen this play out in real life many times, but this one stuck with me. I was at a funeral once when a young couple came to pay their respects. The two seemed to be very sad. They spent a lot of time crying and talking about how they could not eat or sleep because of the loss of their friend's wife.

We were all in sorrow.

But about an hour later, the couple left. We learned they went to a night club right after and partied all night. Were they sad at the funeral? Were they happy at the night club? It's hard to say which was true.

The story ends with the couple breaking up and losing many of their close friends. Their friends didn't forget that the couple abandoned them in their time of need.

Others can tell what you care about by the actions you take.

A leader may show they care about the environment with ceremonial tree planting. A leader may show they care about the elderly by visiting nursing homes and making big donations. Maybe they send Christmas cards and New Year's messages to show appreciation. Maybe they shake hands and say good job when you meet them in hallway.

How much of this outward expression is the real leader, and how much of it is a leader acting like the leader their advisers say people want to have?

People are smart. They will be able to see through an act. The only way a leader can really motivate people and get things done is to be authentic. Pretending gets worse results than not showing any care, love, or respect.

Throughout my career, I dedicated myself to do the job in front of me well, no matter the task assigned to me. At the age of 38, I was a general manager in the USA. Most bosses loved me, and I was their go-to guy.

When I started to get promotions, sometimes my former bosses became my peers, and sometimes I even became their boss. A few of them didn't like the change. They appreciated my drive and the extra work I did when I was their subordinate, but they didn't like me when I was their equal. They saw me as a competitor to be ousted. Most of my former bosses, though, continued to love me and were proud to see me grow.

Their reactions revealed their true nature. How many of them were really dedicated to their employees and invested in seeing them grow? How many of them were in those positions because they enjoyed the prestige? It wasn't hard to tell who was motivated by what.

It's also important to know yourself so you don't fall victim to flattery and manipulation.

Let's say a 25-year-old female acquaintance comes up to you and tells you that you look really handsome and young. But you know you are 60 years old, weigh 200 pounds, and have gray hair. What goes on in your mind when she says that?

That instance isn't any different from when someone approaches you after a town hall meeting to say your speech was great, you are a great leader, and you have dedicated yourself to growing people in the company.

If you know yourself, you won't be blinded by people who are just trying to be nice or who want to get something out of you.

Furthermore, knowing yourself will help you enjoy your role as a leader more. You can express yourself well on your likes and dislikes without worrying about presenting a consistent image. You will be more likely to say yes to things you want to do and to say no even in the midst of social pressure. Self-knowledge will help you to make better decisions about what jobs you should take or reject and whom you should hire or fire to cultivate a cohesive team.

But the most powerful benefit that comes from knowing yourself is that, as a leader, it improves your self-control and self-morale. When you know yourself, you can resist bad habits and develop good habits. You can combat unfairness, dishonesty, and immorality.

In this modern world, we live at a frantic pace. We rarely stop to ask ourselves what we stand for and who we want to be. As a consequence, external demands can dictate our actions if we aren't careful.

## SELF-LEADERSHIP

If someone were to create a manual for life, the first chapter should be on self-leadership. If we can't manage ourselves, we have no business managing others. When you practice self-leadership, you understand who you are, you can identify what you want, and you can intentionally guide yourself toward your goals. Self-leadership determines what you do, why you do it, and how you do it.

So many people spend all their time working and make no time for themselves. When they get closer to retirement, they realize they don't know what they like, so they try to figure it out. Do they like art? Golf? Reading? Traveling?

Those of the industrial age mindset believe work is work and life outside of work is real life. That belief encourages people to do whatever they have to do to keep their job. It means work doesn't need to be a place where they are happy or get fulfillment.

But in the knowledge era, almost all workers, especially those in leadership positions, spend most of their waking hours at the workplace or working. If you subtract the time in a day that you spend sleeping, personal time is really quite limited.

So, to some degree you need to have happiness, satisfaction, and fulfillment at work. It can't be just a place to earn money to have a shot at a better life. That's cheating yourself.

When should one start knowing themselves? Imagine an eight-year-old kid gets into a fight on the playground.

The question "What did you do to make the other kid angry?" might provoke the child to begin getting to know their inner self.

If the parent instead teaches the child to go back the next day and punch the other kid in the face, they are teaching the child to blame others and lash out when things go wrong.

So, the answer to the question above is that one can start to know themselves at a very early age, and it will be a lifetime journey. People are complex. We will continue changing throughout our lives.

Sometimes these changes are small. Once, I had lunch with a friend at the French Concession of Shanghai in China. When the bread and butter was served, my friend mentioned she didn't like butter, so she just started eating the bread.

I was shocked. The butter was so good, I couldn't help but try to persuade her to try it.

Eventually, she humored me. As soon as the butter hit her tongue, her eyes lit up. She loved it so much, we had to order extra.

She had bad butter in the past and convinced herself she didn't like it. Then, she discovered she loved it. As I said, getting to know yourself is a lifelong journey. Your likes and dislikes keep changing.

Your values change too.

Like many other leaders, I started my journey unaware of the power of helping others to grow.

Early in my career, I was an individual contributor, and as a young engineer, what was important to me was getting things done and proving myself at any cost.

As I began moving up in my career and became responsible for large global organizations, I realized the most powerful thing a leader can do is to help people grow. I updated my value system to include promoting growth in people. Some values, such as honesty and fairness, should remain unchanged, but bringing in new values as you learn and grow yourself is required.

Here is a practical approach to self-leadership:

To learn more about yourself, ask three simple questions about your own past, present, and future.
How did I get here from where I started?
Where am I today?
Where do I want to be in the future?

In your own style, write down the answer to these questions. No one else is going to read this, so be honest with yourself.

When you answer the question "How did I get here from where I started?" write down what you did, how you did what you did, and why you did what you did. Do the same with the other questions.

If you haven't thought much about getting to know yourself, those questions are a good place to start. Answering them will help you on your quest for self-leadership.

Some things may be easy to visualize. Maybe you can easily picture your achievements in your career, life, society, family, education, and more.

But the why is most important. Take time to examine your heart and discover the real values and motivations behind your goals. Be honest with yourself.

When you dig into the "how" part, you will discover your likes, dislikes, what you enjoy, what you don't, your strengths, your weaknesses, and more.

Knowing yourself will help you do the right thing in the present moment. You can focus and sense yourself. This is mindfulness, and it will help improve your productivity and do the right things so that you don't have to regret the choices you make in the future.

As you continue to learn and adapt, your values and motivations will adapt too. What you write down here as self-leadership development is also a living document you can and should continually update. That's why in the SIILA model internalization is not a one-time event.

## GOOD VALUES FOR A LEADER

There is no shortage of books and teachings to illustrate good values for a leader. And such books and teachings are not new.

According to *Dasa Raja Dhamma*, or *10 Royal Virtues*, there are 10 values that make for a successful leader. They are generosity, high moral character, making sacrifices for the good of people, kindness, keeping senses under control, being free from hatred, nonviolence, patience, and not opposing the will of people.[53]

According to Confucian theory, Kong Fu Tze once said that when a prince's personal conduct is correct, his government is effective without issuing orders.[54] If his personal conduct is not correct, he may issue orders, but they will not be followed. The idea essentially means the leader should be the role model. As effective leaders, they should demonstrate discipline to positively affect people rather than giving orders.

In *The Art of War,* Sun Tzu explained that leaders must be held accountable to get things done.[55] When there is failure—in his case, losing a war—the root cause comes down to one of five faults of the general, including recklessness, which leads to destruction; cowardice, which leads to capture by enemies; hasty temper, which can be provoked by insults; delicacy of honor, which is sensitive to shame or love-solicitude for his men, which exposes him to worry and trouble.

All those books and pieces of advice are 2,500 years old. The words endure because they are true.

The biggest challenge we face isn't discovering new values to add to our repertoire. We can add new values, such as diversity and environmental protection, but many of our values will remain the same over time because they are good values.

The real challenge is continually internalizing these values and living them out.

## PART III REVIEW

In part III, we discussed internalization of the SIILA model in tackling complexity. Here are the key takeaways:

- When leaders have the right mindset, it improves their productivity and leads them to do the right things unconsciously.
- The journey of finding yourself and discovering who you are is a lifelong journey. When leaders know themselves, they will enjoy their role as a leader and make better decisions.
- The process of internalization helps leaders discover why they want to be a leader and what they want in life so that their actions will be dictated by their inner voice and not by external demands.

The next part of the book will focus on tough-love interactions with others, both inside and outside of the organization.

# PART IV
# INTERACT

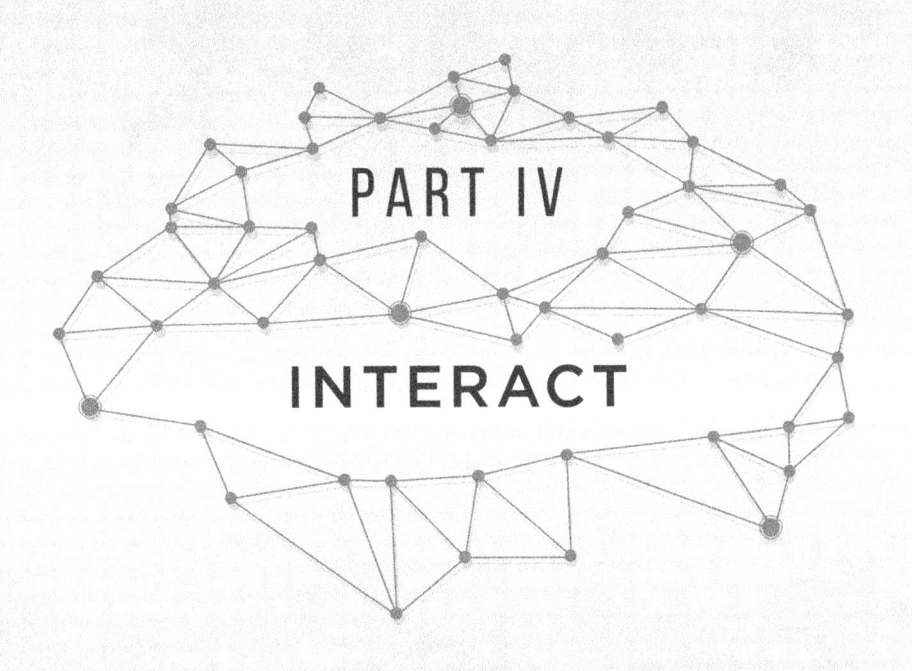

# CHAPTER 7

# WHY TOUGH-LOVE INTERACTIONS ARE WORTH MORE THAN GOLD

Before we dig too deep into the art and science of tough-love interactions and how they are vital to getting things done as a leader, we first need to examine why it's important to get out and see for yourself what's going on.

The following story may help set the stage.

Prince Siddhartha was born to a royal family 600 years before Jesus Christ in the territories south of the Himalayas in Nepal. When the prince was born, the king did everything in his power to provide comfort and protection for his son. In doing so, he forbade the prince from going beyond the walls surrounding the royal palace. The king worried the prince would see all the real suffering in the world and be unhappy.

Eventually, the prince grew curious about the outside world. At the age of 29, the prince convinced a palace helper to take him beyond the walls to see what was out there.

On his journey, the prince saw four sights: an old man, a sick man, a dead man, and an ascetic.

He'd never seen suffering like that before. He realized he lived in a fantasy world at the palace, insulated from the real world. So, he ran away from the palace in search of the truth—eventually finding it and attaining enlightenment.

If this story sounds familiar, it's because it's the story of Buddha. Whether or not the story is true and whether or not you believe in the teachings don't matter here. The story points to an important truth: if the prince had stayed within the palace walls, he never would have known the real world.

That truth often happens in the business world too.

Many leaders today get into trouble when they fail to see the realities on the ground. If others around them work to keep leaders insulated from the truth in order to keep the leaders happy, leaders won't see the real causes of major problems later in their organizations.

If leaders today want to get things done, they need to face these problems, not stay away from them.

There are two main reasons why leaders do not know the truth about their organizations and businesses. Either

- leaders do not want to know the real situation, or
- people around the leader choose to shield the leader from the truth, just like the wall around the prince.

One of the basic principles of the Toyota Production System that makes it so successful is "*Genchi Genbutsu*," which means "Go and see for yourself."

There is just no good alternative to getting your boots on the ground. Although many companies have tried to copy the Toyota Production System, very few have been successful.

Why?

Too many leaders do not go see what is really going on.

Leaders can easily spend all their time in the boardrooms focusing on the postmortem of past failures or dreaming about the future. When those leaders fail to focus on the now, they will not reach that beautiful, blue-ocean future they are dreaming about. They will also lose the present moment.

To really see the present moment, leaders must telescope the organization.

A telescope is used to see objects, such as the moon and the stars, that are far away. We put our eyes right up against the telescope to see objects that are out of our immediate reach. To telescope an organization, leaders must go deeper into the organization, take what is right in front of them, confront the reality, and set the right course for the future.

This view requires going beyond the walls around you—away from all those well-meaning employees who want to spare you pain and difficulty. That's why I call it a tough love interaction.

It is love because the leader cares about the company doing well and being successful while caring equally about the people in the organization and making them successful as well. It is tough love because it requires you to confront the shortcomings of yourself and everyone you interact with head-on.

You cannot make everyone happy, but when you operate with the value system discussed in the previous chapter, you can work to ensure that you and the people in your organization are successful and deliver on the commitments you make.

Tough love involves a great deal of intention, interactivity, consistency, and intimacy.

## LEADERSHIP AS A CONVERSATION

In early 2012, I was the vice president general manager of Global Engine and Transmission Management at Johnson Electric, based in Hong Kong.

Patrick Wang, the chairman and CEO of Johnson Electric, was dedicated to the growth and sustainability of the company. He'd done two major acquisitions in Europe years before, but those acquisitions did not get to the level of integration and performance he expected.

So, Patrick promoted me to the head of the automotive business division with multiple global business units. I relocated to Bern in Switzerland.

It was a new culture, new territory, and new challenge for me and my family.

On my first day, the outgoing leader arranged a meeting at 11 a.m. to introduce me to the team. But no one showed up or dialed in. I waited in the meeting room with the outgoing leader and the secretary for 25 minutes.

The outgoing leader went on and on, telling me how hard it was to bring the team together and get them aligned. He did not seem to have any solutions for the problem.

On my way back to the office, I asked the secretary what was really going on.

"This place needs discipline," she said.

Right away I was confronted with the first problem I had to tackle. It made sense—they brought me in to fix problems, after all. I decided there was no point in blaming others or pointing fingers. I just got to work.

I called all the vice presidents of the business units and the functions who were supposed to report to me and attend the call that day. I had good individual conversations with all of them and set up a Monday-morning, weekly leadership meeting all were expected to attend at 9 a.m. sharp.

That Monday, everyone showed up on time. From there on out, no one ever delayed the meeting, even by a minute. They could tell I took it seriously, so they did too. Taking that time to connect with personal interactions and genuine intentions began to lead to real intimacy.

Finally, all of us could start to get on the same page. We created a forum to stay connected with each other and work together to resolve issues

## WHY TOUGH-LOVE INTERACTIONS ARE WORTH MORE THAN GOLD

that came up. We improved the organization's performance and improved the discipline that the secretary said the company needed.

Five weeks later, Patrick came to visit me. He said the level of integration at the company in the last five weeks had been better than what he had seen in five years.

That may have been an overstatement, but you get the idea. Transformation can happen fast when leaders use personal interactions and genuine intentions.

From there, we dug even deeper.

After the 9 a.m. meeting with my direct reports, I instituted an escalation meeting. For the next two hours, I listened to problems being dealt with by larger groups in the company.

Leadership meetings helped me to reiterate the organization's values and priorities and to listen to my direct reports on the major updates aligning the team.

Escalation meetings helped me to telescope how things happened in the deeper organization. The concerns could be problems ranging from quality issues, to material shortages, to new-program launch delays, to customer delivery issues, to financial performance issues that our people needed help with. We worked to confront the issues head-on, together.

These problems often go through many layers of the organization before hitting the top leader, so solving the issue is not hard. But I find the interaction to be a great opportunity to stay in tune with the mindset of the organization that creates these problems. Then I can try to change that mindset.

The leader must be comfortable with the details and depth required to analyze the issues. Gaining such knowledge allows the leader and others in the organization to be more comfortable with smarter, cross-functional solutions.

I like to treat these escalation meetings like case studies. By bringing in the whole team to solve problems and figure out what went wrong, the whole team learns how to stop that problem from happening, and we get more creative solutions.

If, as a leader, you do not welcome discussions around problems and just beat up those who bring issues to your attention, you will be seen as unfit for the job. The organization will emerge to be against you.

In my experience, every time I start a new job, I see a lot of escalation items during those two-hour meetings. We spend a lot of time examining issues and finding solutions. I use them and the time as opportunities to create a mindset around fairness and honesty.

But as time passes, I see fewer and fewer escalation items brought to the table. Why? Because we've gotten to the root of the problem, and my employees feel empowered to enact solutions.

That is how organizations are created to shadow the leader.

Leaders get many opportunities to connect with people, but few take those opportunities.

Corporate communication departments distribute well-written and formatted speeches and emails under a leader's name. But these help very little, if at all, to positively transform the organization. If leaders are too busy and do not have time to have personal interactions with employees, they must be doing something wrong.

Today, large companies are attempting to mimic the approach start-up companies usually take, such as flexibility, loyalty, creativity, team chemistry, and culture. But large companies are not the same as start-ups.

Obviously, the scale tends to be quite different. But leaders also face challenges with lack of alignment, fear in decision-making, power distance, lack of proper feedback on current systems and processes, and more.

One of the biggest advantages start-ups have over large companies is the benefit of personal interactions. When companies are smaller, it is easier to have those interactions—but that doesn't mean larger companies are off the hook. Just because it is harder does not mean leaders of big companies have fewer opportunities. Leaders of companies of all sizes must recognize the value of these personal interactions and then do them right.

There are four key elements for leaders to focus on to make these tough-love interactions happen and get things done in complexity. They are

- intentions,
- consistency,
- interactions, and
- intimacy.

## INTENTIONS

First, the leader's intentions must be very clear. Stay on agenda on your vision, mission, strategy, and values. That concept is simple.

## CONSISTENCY

Second, consistency is really important. It also requires conscious effort. A leader cannot be in one meeting and say he doesn't care about the company's future innovations and is instead prioritizing short-term profits, then next week complain people aren't investing enough on innovations. The organization will become confused, and people will completely lose trust in the leader. Leaders also cannot have favorites. Favoritism ruins consistency. Right is right, and wrong is wrong, regardless of who does it. Treat everyone equally. Sounds simple, but it is harder than you think.

The need for consistency extents to our attitudes too.

Leaders meet with many people every day. A leader may feel tired, frustrated, sleepy, angry, and more. You may have a hundred meetings a day, but that hundredth person, who may be seeing you at 7 p.m. right before you leave the office, is well prepared to see you. It might be their only chance all year to see you.

You can't act tired and frustrated with this person regardless of what happened during the whole busy day before this meeting. It's not fair to them. And it reflects poorly on you.

If you want that employee to go back and create positive emergence in the organization, you must stay consistent. Be in high spirits and focused no matter the time of day or the outcome of your previous meeting.

As we discussed in the chapter on internalizing, if you have internalized why you want to be a leader, you will always be passionate, in high spirits, and have positive energy. You are the mood elevator for the entire organization.

## INTERACTIONS

Third comes the actual interaction part. Leaders must initiate a dialogue, whether formal or informal. Show you care about what you're asking your employee about. Listen to them. Create an environment where employees feel they can speak up.

When employees speak up, it is an opportunity for leaders to get to know the real state of the organization.

Be direct and clear whether you're giving feedback on a large-operation review meeting, conducting a performance review, wishing someone happy birthday, or chatting with someone in the hallway.

## INTIMACY

Do employees always tell leaders the truth?

If employees do not trust the leader, they will never speak the truth—and you will never know the truth. So, you as a leader need to develop that trust with your employees. Show them you do not have a hidden agenda, are not hostile, and deliver on the commitments you make.

Once, I had a boss who wasn't qualified for his job. He had many performance and behavior issues. When he was fired, his boss asked me why I didn't reach out to him and mention those problems earlier.

Well, he didn't ask me. And even if he had, I had no reason to trust him. I was afraid of being characterized as a hostile employee for complaining about his choice in people.

This kind of thing happens everywhere. Leaders must build that intimacy and show they genuinely want the truth.

## CONFRONTING THE BRUTAL REALITIES

It is the leader's job to deal with difficult topics. Leaders make important and deeply consequential decisions every day that affect the short- and long-term existence of their organizations, stakeholders, and employees. Much uncertainty surrounds the decisions leaders make, because no one can predict the future. But given that the chance for making the right decisions drastically goes up when the leaders know the reality of the situation, it's critical that leaders are willing to accept and confront those brutal realities.

Ford Motor Company was bleeding money and deep in the red when Alan Mulally became the CEO in 2006. That year, Ford lost $12.7 billion—even more than the previous year's $10.6 billion loss.[56]

Despite the long-standing motto Quality Is Job One, Ford faced massive field-quality issues with more than nine recalls on the subcompact Ford Focus and poor-quality ratings for Freestar and Windstar minivans. At the time, individual brands within Ford and its separate geographies were operating in a highly autonomous manner with less global connectivity, meaning the company was far from unified in its efforts.

Before joining Ford, Mulally was the executive vice president of The Boeing Company and president and chief executive officer of Boeing Commercial Airplanes.

Bill Ford, CEO of Ford prior to Mulally, attempted several times to turn around the company, including workforce reductions and plant closings, but he failed. So, the company turned to a leader outside to help Ford turn the tide.

Mulally came in as an outsider. He asked innocent questions to learn and understand the real issues. When he did, he decided to confront the reality of what was before him. He understood what a task it was to turn around this broken company.

His strategy was One Ford, so he took action to divest the other brands except Ford and Lincoln.

He raised money for the turnaround while two other Detroit giants, General Motors and Chrysler, had to get a bailout from the U.S. government during the great recession.

Mulally went deep into the details to fix quality issues. He worked to connect the organization as one team globally and improved performance in a new management process known as the business plan review.

Every Thursday, Ford's entire global leadership was required to attend a virtual meeting. Video conferencing facilities were installed at each location so that the team could experience being together and have meaningful interactions.

These meetings gave Mulally a practical, hands-on platform to add management discipline to the One Ford strategy.[57]

From around the world, the team brought issues to the forefront, discussed them, and resolved them.

Like the escalation meetings I have with my own team, Mulally's meetings were about more than issue resolution. They were critical for Mulally to telescope the company and develop a thriving culture and mindset within the organization. With these changes, positive patterns emerged.

Sticking to the path is tough and requires the leader to be well disciplined, engaged, and invested—all while following up with action and staying consistent.

Mulally's process worked. In 2014, eight years after Mulally took over, Ford reported a $6.8 billion profit. Today, Mulally is recognized as the man who pulled off one of the greatest turnarounds in business history.[58]

Although a great vision and strategy is important, that alone is not enough. A leader's ability and willingness to see the reality and confront it through tough-love interactions are the ultimate tools necessary to get things done in complexity.

In large organizations, it may be impossible for leaders to interact with every single person. If that's the case, leaders must invest in other leaders throughout the organization, developing them into good role models who do have these cascading interactions with their subordinates.

In the next chapter, we'll talk about who is really on your team and why it's important to know the leaders you hire to work for you. Remember, they will often be the ones leading and interacting with your employees.

# CHAPTER 8

# KNOW WHO'S REALLY ON YOUR TEAM

Julius Caesar's death may just be one of the most well-known, dramatic, violent, bloody scenes out there. In case you somehow managed to avoid hearing the tale, a group of senators—among them one of Caesar's closest allies, Brutus—ganged up to stab Julius Caesar to death. Then they washed their hands of his blood. Just before collapsing and breathing his last breath, Julius Caesar looked at Brutus, surprised by the betrayal. Looking into Brutus' eyes, Julius Caesar uttered: *"Et tu, Brute?"*

This literally means "Even you, Brutus?"

It's not clear whether Brutus was actually Julius Caesar's son or just a close ally, but Caesar may have helped to raise the boy. He trusted Brutus, and he could not believe Brutus could betray him.[59]

We can learn from this story by taking the lessons here and applying them to the business environment.

## TACKLING COMPLEXITY

Today, when leaders fail to deliver on their commitments, most will say they hired the wrong person or trusted the wrong person to get the job done.

It's true that leaders get into trouble when they trust the wrong person—be it by betrayal or being incapable to get things done. It may be that some of the people closest to and most trusted by the leader cause the leader to fail.

If you haven't already, you will hear many consultants and advisers speak about having the right person in the right job as a competitive advantage. Their advice is absolutely true. The right person in the right job is part of the formula to win. Getting it done and knowing the right person to do it is the challenge. With this in mind, remember to ask yourself these two questions:

- Do you really know this person?
- Even if you do know them now, people keep changing. Are they changing for the better or worse?

Those questions pose a big challenge for even the most renowned leaders out there. Warren Buffett even spoke about the importance of hiring the right people—and how hard it can be to do so.

"You get a guy or a woman in charge of it—they're personable, the directors like 'em—they don't know what they're doing. But they know how to put on an appearance. That's the biggest single danger."[60]

Here is the fundamental problem.

Some people master how to make a good show, present themselves really well, and make bosses and directors like them, but they can't actually get things done. Having a leader like that is the biggest single danger for an organization.

But it's not necessarily easy to spot these people.

Remember, people are complex, and people change. They may love you today and decide they hate you tomorrow. They may have been good in the past, but that doesn't mean they will continue to be good. You won't get to know your people during the interview process. It's a lifelong journey.

I've made mistakes in this area too.

Once, I started a new role as president of a business and had an employee reporting to me whom other corporate leaders didn't like. Let's call him Bob. Those corporate leaders wanted to fire him. But I liked him, so I moved him to another job to save him.

He often traveled with me to meet with customers, and we did a lot of good things together to turn around the business. He was pleasant, polished, and always wore the most expensive suit among my executive team. If you talked to him, you loved him. We were friends for years. He and his wife often came over to my house to have dinner with my wife and me.

But eventually I got the sense he wasn't being honest.

It all came to a head when we were scheduled to go to Silicon Valley for a business trip. We had traveled together many times before, but this time he told me he didn't want to take the same flight as mine because it was too expensive. I sensed something was wrong then, but I decided to keep quiet.

Later, I learned he left for San Francisco four days before I did.

We'd planned to have lunch the day I arrived, so I waited for his call. And waited and waited. It didn't come.

I asked him about it later, and he told me his flight got delayed—but I knew he checked into the same hotel the same day I did, from wherever he had stayed the previous four days.

We met for dinner as we usually did on business trips. As usual, I suggested we sit down in the lobby for a drink as we prepared for the next day's meeting. But he said he was too tired and wanted to go back to sleep. We'd traveled together probably a hundred times before, and he had never acted like this.

Eventually, we came to learn that he had brought his mistress with him on the trip, which explained the separate flight, the skipped lunch, and the rush back to his room.

I'm not here to pass judgment on his personal choices regarding the mistress. That's not my call to make. But during this trip, patterns of dishonesty and poor integrity emerged. There were enough signals for me to know where this emergence was heading.

I had a tough, direct conversation with him about it after we returned to the office. I thought we fixed the problem, but he was a master of appearances, and I was wrong.

I discovered that he had been telling customers I didn't want to or didn't have time to visit with them when they asked for an executive meeting. He blocked my messages from getting through to his organization and asked the team not to pay attention to my requests. He lied about business matters too.

We had to let him go despite the fact he was able to claim the best commercial performance among the group at the time. It was so hard to know who he really was because he mastered the image of a good employee and a good friend.

When this all happened, I felt the phrase *Et tu, Brute* to my core, because I had trusted, protected, and mentored this man.

So, how do you accurately measure performance to make sure something like that doesn't happen? It's important to have perspective.

If you have one of the best leaders in the industry and you put them on a really difficult task, the results may look average. If you put an average leader on a really easy task, the results may look fantastic.

If you spend too much time praising the average leaders for finishing an easy task and punishing the best leaders for pulling off a difficult task, your good leaders will quit.

How do you know what your people really do?

If you rely on the charts those leaders present, you may miss the bigger picture. Average leaders may be hiding the truth and telling you only what you want to hear. They may be masking bad behaviors and feigning integrity. Check in on their real work and behavior on an ongoing basis—otherwise, you won't know who the real Bob is.

It's not that you shouldn't trust your people. It's that you know people are complex and they change. You know you must continually interact with them in all possible ways, which means going beyond the boardroom.

## FORGIVE BUT NEVER FORGET

People make mistakes. That's an inevitable part of being human, and you can't avoid it when you employ people in a complex system. When people make mistakes, forgiving them and helping them to improve strengthens relationships and improves emotional health.

But as the old saying goes, fool me once, shame on you; fool me twice, shame on me. Forgiving someone for their past mistakes doesn't mean you have to forget what they did—whether that was bungling a financial report or lying about their work.

Unless people learn from their mistakes and make improvements, they will eventually fail you again.

Forgiving but not forgetting allows you to see emerging patterns that can lead to bigger problems.

When Bob lied about his flight, missed lunch, and rushed back to his room, there was a pattern of manipulation that stretched from his personal matters into business matters. If it were allowed to continue, he could have caused major problems for the company. If I would have looked the other way, it either could have signaled to other employees that this behavior was okay, or it could have eroded trust with employees who knew that what he was doing was wrong. Neither outcome helps you get things done, and that leader will eventually fail.

Your ability to have these tough-love interactions is what makes the organization better. If you put off having those conversations or confronting those problems, you will gain a reputation for being either easily fooled or a pushover—neither of which positions you to be a leader respected by your organization.

# TACKLING COMPLEXITY

## TELESCOPING BEHAVIOR AND PERFORMANCE

Crisis prevention is always top of mind for successful leaders. They know that when big failures happen, it's too late to fix the problem. At that point, it won't matter if you forgive the other person for making a big mistake—you might lose your job first.

If Dennis Muilenburg learned his team at Boeing was taking safety risks due to cost cutting pressures earlier on, he could have forgiven them and corrected the behavior. But he either didn't know or chose to ignore the problem, and as a result, two planes crashed. It was too late for the CEO to forgive mistakes because he already lost his job.

Why don't leaders see what's really going on?

When leaders refuse to telescope behavior and go deeper to understand the people who work for them, they are blind to what's happening around them. And many leaders out there simply refuse to do the work involved to telescope their people.

Once, a CEO came to one of my manufacturing plants totally unannounced. He was in the area and had some free time, so he stopped by. He walked around the shop floor, went to the worker's washrooms, walked to the engineering labs, and talked to some people.

In the following month's regular business review, he told everyone that I ran a good business. He went on to say the workers' facilities, discipline, and behavior were highly commendable and that other business leaders should learn from it.

That was a nice surprise. I didn't view his visit as his micromanaging me or my employees or his lacking trust in me. I had nothing to hide, and I felt good enough about my organization that my doors were always open for my bosses to visit.

When leaders do announce their visits, they are often given the VIP welcome. They get the red-carpet rollout, the five-star hotel, the catered food, and the shiny washrooms. They get escorts to make sure they don't see anything unsightly. They don't see the reality of the situation, much like the prince who grew up with the walls around him whom we discussed last chapter.

Good leaders should commit to eating the normal-employee food, using the normal washrooms, talking to operators, engaging with young employees, and walking around. You'd be surprised how much more you can learn about local leadership by doing those things than you do in a meeting room reviewing PowerPoint presentations.

Being present regularly is a good opportunity for you to observe and get to know your people as they do the work in real time. Ask questions. Keep your senses open. This isn't about trying to catch your employees doing something wrong. It isn't about doubting your people. This is about you being accountable for getting things done and making people better.

Those actions are part of tough-love interactions. I ask my people questions, I observe them, and I always provide direct, sometimes painful, feedback. That's tough love. But when you have built trust and credibility with your people, it's hard for anyone to have hard feelings. They know it's for the benefit of everyone.

I take those actions for two reasons:

- I am accountable for delivering on my commitments.
- I am responsible for making my people better.

## LEAD WITH A HEALTHY IMAGE

At this point, you know you need to be honest and direct in your interactions. There's just no sugarcoating it. Leaders must be willing to confront the brutal realities in front of them.

That being said, you have to practice what you preach. You must be a role model to inspire your people and for them to follow you. Otherwise, you will see negative emergence.

As a leader, I've taken many risks and I've made some tough decisions. People didn't always respond well. Some wrote to my higher-ups complaining about me, some threatened my life, and some tried to sue me. Although leaders try everything possible to avoid those measures, the reality is they happen.

I worked with Bob for five years. We traveled around the world on business trips, and I considered him a friend. But I had no issue letting him go. I wasn't afraid to when it was clear I had to.

But imagine what would have happened if we'd done something illegal together and he had proof of it. What if he had secret pictures, recordings, or proof I'd committed fraud? I never would have been able to make those tough decisions and follow through. He would have been in control.

When you are in a leadership position, there are always opportunities for temptation. These opportunities may take the shape of accepting or giving bribes, having personal affairs, or manipulating financial reports. If you start doing one small thing, it becomes hard to stop. And when such actions involve other people, you lose control. They are in charge now because they know your secrets. The solution here is don't start. Anchor back to your value system.

Control your temptations. Remember, we came here after finding out who we are and internalizing why we wanted to be leaders in the first place.

So, it's important to stay clean and lead with a healthy image. When you don't have secrets and haven't done anything wrong, you have courage and power. You don't have to fear internal investigations or legal cases. Instead of being bad, those investigations against you become an opportunity to prove to the world you are clean and run a good business.

In the next chapter, we will talk about the importance of interactions cutting across boundaries within your own organization and outside of it.

# CHAPTER 9

# HOW TO BREAK DOWN SILOS AND BUILD UP TEAMS

Physical, mental, and emotional walls create personal boundaries to protect us from being used or manipulated by others. Everyone has such barriers. When these boundaries are well managed, we feel good about ourselves.

Boundaries happen at the workplace too.

Within organizations, there are countless boundaries from procedures and policies to vertical and horizontal organization charts, business units, functions, corporate, managers, prototype shops, and mass-production sites. These boundary lines are also managed and enforced to protect the leader as the primary objective.

It is impossible to have a healthy relationship without strong and clear boundaries. That reality applies to you and your mother-in-law as much as it does for design engineers and production managers.

But all too often, we forget that a boundary line shouldn't be the same thing as a silo.

Almost all value-creation activities taken to accelerate overall performance require cutting across boundary lines at appropriate moments.

Leaders build organizations with boundaries in mind to help make work more manageable. Such boundaries typically take the form of different manufacturing plants, business units, project teams, and functions.

Although such separation is desirable, leaders today are challenged with finding ways to cut across those boundary lines when necessary to accomplish a larger mission or improve performance. These boundary-spanning efforts require an organization to build bridges between silos to facilitate the flow of information across boundary lines.

That concept works in theory. How does it look in real life?

Let's stay on the line of interactions. In chapters 7 and 8, we saw how a successful leader goes beyond the walls to see the reality, take on tough conversations, confront realities, and telescope to know that his team and the right people are on the right jobs doing the right things. These interaction efforts are boundary-spanning interactions.

## CLARITY OF PURPOSE

When I was the head of a global automotive business based in Switzerland, I encountered a problem that serves as a perfect fit for our conversation on cutting across boundary lines.

One particular business unit had its engineering design center centralized in Switzerland. One particular customer was located in Detroit in the United States. When I visited our regional office in Detroit, the team loudly complained about working with the Swiss.

"The Swiss are too slow," the team said. They were very frustrated and afraid that slowness could lead to losing a large business.

I had no idea what they were talking about.

In my experience, Switzerland was a country full of people who were super punctual. Beyond that, the particular products were highly engineered and could not afford to be designed in multiple regions; therefore, they had to be centralized in Switzerland where historical know-how existed to serve a global customer base. Even if the Detroit office was frustrated, they couldn't design these products by themselves and had to continue serving their customers' day-to-day needs.

Something had to give. I recognized that multiple boundaries were at play here. There were two countries, two cultures, a design center, a sales office, customers, and more. Unless I confronted this reality right at that moment, everyone would continue to protect their boundaries, and the issue would just escalate. Making a big speech that we were one team and that we must work together wouldn't help to address the frustrations of the people on the ground and deliver on commitments.

I told the team this: "I don't know if the Swiss are too slow or not. If they are, I can't fix that problem. Changing the whole culture of a country is too big for me."

But I could remove that kind of high-level, country- and culture-wide language barrier and bring clarity to the discussion.

What if instead the U.S. sales team said, "The Swiss engineering team committed to deliver five prototypes on April 15, but today is April 20, and we still don't have the prototypes. What happened?"

Then I could find out what happened.

I could solve this problem. This communication brings clarity around the who, what, when, and why of a commitment.

The fix may sound like a very simple solution—and it's definitely easier than making all Swiss people move faster—but it's powerful. It cut across many different boundary lines and silos to bring clarity to the discussion and focus on getting things done and delivering on commitments. Project managers were able to start a new action-reporting format and follow up and escalate if they need help. The team performance improved, and we launched projects successfully.

Within a boundary, people tend to understand each other very well. By the nature of the boundary itself, we don't quite understand what goes on outside our boundary. The best approach is to bring clarity in one common language.

Write down your commitment, agree on it, and talk through it to make sure there is no ambiguity around it.

If someone changes the plan or is unable to deliver on their commitments, we can deal with that as discussed in previous chapters, whether it's a one-off or a new emerging pattern.

But you must begin with clarity.

How does clarity look with respect to working with customers and suppliers?

## WEAK LINKS IN THE SUPPLY CHAIN

Let's take a look at the semiconductor supply chain issue again. The entire process involves transforming wafers of silicon into a network of billions of tiny switches called transistors that eventually are integrated into functioning circuits. This process could take three to six months, and they travel several times between continents before they get assembled into cars, mobile phones, washing machines, and more.

The world faced a semiconductor shortage in 2021 due to the entire supply chain's inability to get aligned on the deliveries. Customers increased demand, but the supply chain lacked capacity. This process involves a multitier supply chain, and many companies are involved. Clearly, they all have their own boundary lines.

When leaders in this industry do not interact outside their own boundary lines and do not work to bring clarity to the situation, supply chain issues are unavoidable.

I experienced a similar issue once.

A customer suddenly increased the volume in their order, by a lot. To produce those products for the customer, my team had to get parts from our suppliers at a cost of $5 million—with expedited airfreight versus the normal sea freight.

Well, $5 million is a big number. I refused to absorb the sudden airfreight cost, and the customer pushed back, threatening to take business away.

In regular production, customers have order windows, and that order has to come with a certain amount of lead time to guarantee deliveries. If orders are made suddenly and unexpectedly, it jams up the supply chain.

This order was sudden. The customer asked us to deliver significantly more parts in a span of several weeks. That volume was something we didn't plan for and wasn't reasonably possible.

I sensed a bigger backstory. Plus, if I had to blindly accept an unexpected $5 million airfreight fee, I would be on the hook for falling short on my own commitments for financial performance for the company. In this case, the entire value chain would lose money—except, of course, the express courier service.

With the pressure building from the customer, I committed to a boundary-spanning interaction. When the issue got escalated, I asked the customer executives how the problem happened. Did they just decide to suddenly build so many more cars? How did they not anticipate the need earlier?

We later learned that another supplier failed to deliver to the customer on time, so the customer switched its order with us.

Although a new order sounded good on paper, the switch meant we would lose more money than the revenue we would bring in if we paid the $5 million airfreight charge. So, I refused the deal. It didn't make sense for us to lose money just because the customer chose an incapable supplier first.

This example uses a system created by the leader in boundary-spanning interactions to escalate issues that are negatively affecting the business, with the leader being willing to dig into the details, ask questions to understand the purpose, and demand clarity.

Boundaries can protect people and make job distinctions clear, but if they aren't managed well, they can bring negative value. If the $5 million airfreight cost was just accepted without question, the company would have suffered.

It's no wonder so many customers sue suppliers and suppliers sue customers. There is an abundance of poor-quality products and services, missing deliveries, late orders, and broken contracts.

Systems thinking protects you from this chaos. It helps you to understand the interconnectivity and the emergence, making it clear that everyone in the system, from the customer to the supplier, is important. If the customer is hurting the suppliers or the suppliers are hurting the customers, the system will not be successful. There must be honest, trust-based, transparent conversations to ensure everyone wins. If systems thinking is internalized by all the parties, a peaceful settlement and solution are possible.

## BROKEN WINDOWS THEORY

In chapter 1, we saw how Airbus and Boeing both had new product launches that faced massive, expensive delays. Paying penalties to customers and losing money is the last step in a project gone wrong.

More of their manufacturing than ever before was outsourced to suppliers both locally and internationally. The approach was intended to significantly reduce development time and cost. However, results yielded the opposite. Multitudes of issues arose with systems coordination, outsourcing, supplier oversight, and global communication, all while launching significantly new technologies. Ultimately, the programs saw multiple delays, launching years behind schedule, and had to deal with postlaunch design and quality problems.[61]

There were enough early signs that bad things were on the way before the launches were delayed and costs went way over the budget. Similarly, we see many companies lose on financial commitments because they either lose sales or costs are out of control.

But what are the early signs these big issues will happen?

You may have heard of the term *broken windows theory*. It's an idea that suggests visible signs of disorder and misbehavior in an environment lead to further disorder and misbehavior, which lead to serious crimes.[62]

We can apply this concept to the business environment.

If you, as a leader, aren't seeing the broken-windows issues and only learn of the major disasters, you won't be able to prevent those disasters. So, why aren't you seeing the broken windows and preventing disasters from happening?

I can think of two reasons why leaders don't see these broken windows in their organizations: (1) the organization does not have confidence that escalating issues to the leader will get the problem resolved, and (2) instead, it will create more work, more reviews, and more blame.

People don't understand that small things can lead to big problems.

Either way, leaders need to position themselves as the go-to people to get problems resolved.

Most of the time, if an issue is contained to one boundary line, the head of that department will resolve the problem. But organizations tend to slow down when the problem involves multiple boundaries and requires different groups to work together from multiple regions, functions, business units, or corporate management.

Throughout my general management career, I avoided major issues by creating space to sense risks and escalate them early so we could resolve them before problems got big.

## ESCALATION BUSINESS SCHOOL

On December 26, 2004, a tsunami from the Indian Ocean killed nearly 300,000 people in 14 countries. It was a massive tragedy.[63]

As the tsunami approached shorelines, water receded from the coast, exposing the ocean floor. Animals sensed the disaster. Elephants trumpeted and ran for higher ground. Dogs refused to go outside. Flamingoes refused to lay eggs on low-lying breeding areas. But humans gathered to see the strange water levels. Some went out to play on the extended beaches and look at the exposed fish. But when the water started rushing back, many people died.

What happened to the sensing capabilities of humans?

Imagine there is a system within an organization to sense trouble that will eventually lead to big disasters if it isn't resolved early. Just like a typhoon warning or hurricane severity indicator, you would know exactly how much attention to give a particular problem.

If you're like me, you'd be willing to pay a nice fee for such a system. Let's create it.

Imagine issues are classified as L1, L2, L3, and L4.

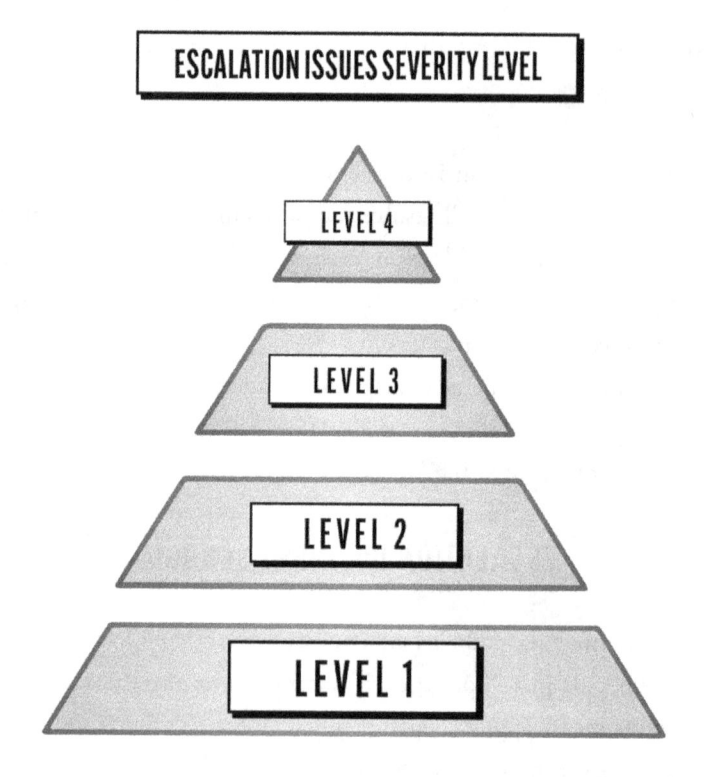

**ESCALATION ISSUES SEVERITY LEVEL**

- LEVEL 4
- LEVEL 3
- LEVEL 2
- LEVEL 1

First-level managers can resolve L1 issues. Functional leads can take care of L2. At L3, the executive committee or your direct reports need to get engaged. At L4, you own them. You cannot delegate them to anyone else.

When I first created the escalation meetings, so many L1, L2, and L3 escalations came to my attention—and others had the chance to watch how I handled it. I dug into the root cause, asked detailed questions, and worked to help with specific technical fixes and the system issues that caused the problem.

People watched and learned, so the number of escalation cases I helped with went down. Today, many of the issues get resolved at L2 and L3 rather than getting all the way up to L4. That's the power of boundary-spanning interactions. You can create a system to sense the severity level of the signals in the organizational mind and make it self-calibrating. For leaders, every opportunity is perfect to interact and create a positive emergence to make the organization work and achieve its goals.

For leaders, it's not about solving these individual issues. Of course, they must be comfortable with solving issues. It's about knowing the organization, finding bad patterns, and fixing them with the right interactions.

The example I used earlier regarding the $5 million airfreight cost has been observed by many of my managers. What did they learn from it? How would they share the message with others in the organization? Bringing them into the conversation to see how I handled it created a big impact.

When an issue gets to your level, you are the leader who has all the authority and resources to get the problem resolved, so of course it gets resolved. But your focus should not only be on fixing the problem but on making the organization better so that similar problems don't happen again. That is the power of these interactions.

As a leader, how can you make sure this happens? Here are some key takeaways:

- Focus on learning and not just fixing the problem.
- Make data-driven decisions and keep discussions based on facts Keep emotions away.

- Demonstrate organizational interconnectivity with boundary-spanning interactions.
- Don't be afraid of tough issues.
- Turn problems into a business school case study discussion.

Let's go back to the $5 million airfreight issue for a moment.

First, ask questions. When the issue was brought to my attention, I started asking questions to learn more. Why was there a sudden demand increase? What was the profitability of this account? If we paid this cost, what would be the profitability?

These questions will make the people around you realize what kind of details and data should be analyzed to figure out the best course of action. I focused on learning here rather than just solving the problem so my people would know what to do the next time something like it happened. This creates a positive emergence.

Second, ask for data and keep the discussion rooted in facts, both of which help take the emotions out. You don't want to have things like "this customer is good" or "this supplier is bad" factor into the discussion. Keep the facts of the deal—like our company being poised to lose more money than it would bring in on this deal—front and center.

Third, get others engaged by showing them how the organization works. Get other functions to come in and help to resolve issues and create value. Bring in cross-functional expertise. Be sure people on the ground see you hold top guys accountable and expect them to know the details. Do not beat up junior people and protect the big buys. It should be other way around. Hold senior staff in your direct reports accountable. Then, they will be serious and will avoid another similar issue happening again.

Fourth, don't be afraid of tough issues. Face that brutal reality. Confront it. Cleaning out the rubbish may be ugly, but once done, it's clean. Don't close the meeting if you still have real, difficult issues and conversations you need to tackle. Just get right in and take care of it.

Fifth, turn everything into a business school case study discussion. Ask others to jump in and advise or comment. Many business schools today teach their MBA students using case studies. Isn't your own real-life experience the perfect opportunity to create a case study discussion? There will be a great level of participation and interest from others because it's something tangible they can learn from. Next time, they will have similar discussions without you, and they will get good at analyzing and solving issues.

With those top five specific focus areas in boundary-spanning interactions, leaders must continue to demonstrate the basic qualities of interactions we discussed in chapter 7, including right intentions, consistency, positive interactions, and intimacy.

We discussed tough-love interactions within your organization as well as outside the boundary lines we tend to draw within our own silos. The real power of the interactions is that you begin to learn what you don't know.

# PART IV REVIEW

In part IV, we discussed tough-love interactions of the SIILA model in tackling complexity. Here are the key takeaways:

- With tough-love interactions, leaders have the ability to telescope the organization, to *go see,* to learn the real status of the organization, sense issues that could create problems later, and proactively address the issues when they are still small in order to avoid major failures.
- Having the right people in the right job is a competitive advantage for organizations, but in practice, leaders must continue to get engaged and get to know their people in order to get a sense of who they are and how they are changing.
- Leaders must be comfortable interacting with everyone inside and outside the organization to learn about and create organizational sensitivity, solve escalation issues, and create positive emergence.

With tough-love interactions, you know what you don't know—you identify the knowledge gap. The next part of this book on the SIILA model is learn.

# PART V

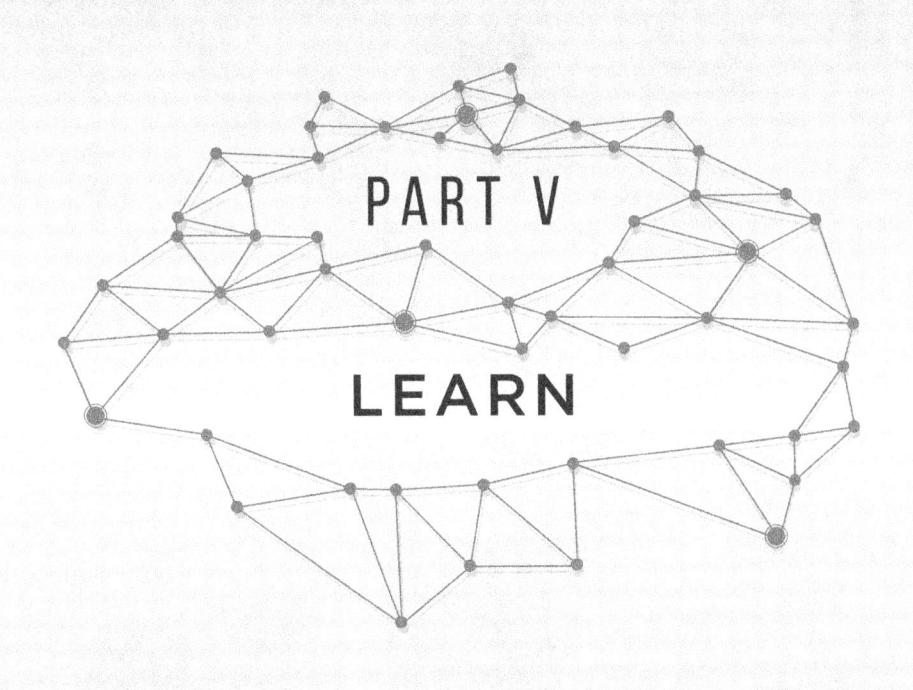

# LEARN

# CHAPTER 10

# HOW LEADERS BEGIN TO LEARN WITH TOUGH-LOVE INTERACTIONS

Leadership titles are some of the most envied positions out there. From manager to CEO, millions of people line up to claim that role. I get it. Leaders look as if they have a lot of power, as if they have status, and as if they are competent in all they do.

But that notion is far from the truth. Successful leaders are always on the hunt for more knowledge and trying to improve their skills. Deep inside, leaders know there is so much they don't know, and they worry those unknowns could lead to failure. Leaders are under pressure to get things done and deliver. To do so well, a leader must recognize that they must develop a lifelong love of learning.

In tackling complexity, learning is the most important skill. Every other skill will become obsolete over time, but the skill of learning will serve you for however long you use it.

So, are leaders supposed to learn how to do every little thing within an organization? No. That's impossible. But they are expected to do certain things well, including hiring, integration, and managing the operation with their own team.

These expectations are easier said than done, of course.

But the crux of it is this: Leadership is all about coping with complexity. In the complexity paradigm, a leader can be certain that the people, the organization, the culture, the customers, the suppliers, the markets, etc. will change and keep changing.

Tackling complexity is not about the technical skills of capital budgeting or managing people in a command-and-control leadership style. In complexity, leadership is about modeling the right values and behavior, setting the direction, and aligning the organization toward one common goal even during uncertain times. Leaders will know they have succeeded when they can do all that *and* deliver on their commitments.

To do this, leaders must identify their knowledge gaps in two broad categories. Yes, every leader has them. The categories are interconnected—just like everything else we've talked about—but for clarity, let's talk about them separately.

They are the technical knowledge gap and the organizational knowledge gap.

## TECHNICAL KNOWLEDGE GAP

Imagine for a moment a three-year-old asks his dad why their car cannot fly. It's one of those questions where it doesn't do anyone any good to go into too much detail. Can the father explain gravity, physics, aerodynamics, and more in a way the three-year-old will understand?

Probably not. So, he simply says the car can't fly because it doesn't have wings. That's good enough for the three-year-old. He understands that.

What does this example have to do with the leadership world? Quite a lot, actually.

## HOW LEADERS BEGIN TO LEARN WITH TOUGH-LOVE INTERACTIONS

Now, before the leaders reading this book get angry that I just compared them to a child, think of it this way: Compared to a product design engineer, you probably *do* have the understanding of a child. That's okay. It's not your job to understand how each and every product is designed.

And if you don't keep this in mind when you work with people in your business, you might come away looking worse than a child. You might look like an idiot.

Let's look at a real-life example.

At one point, the board of directors at a company I worked for appointed a new president to an automotive engine business. In a meeting, the new leader, let's call him Ted, challenged the ignition coil business unit leader, let's call him Bill.

Ted said Bill was not a capable leader. He said Bill wasn't growing the business fast enough, and he recommended Bill start selling ignition coils to the diesel engine manufacturers instead of always focusing on gasoline engine manufacturers. Ted said that was the kind of out-of-the-box thinking the company needed to sell more products, create new markets, and grow the company.

If you, like Ted, don't know anything about cars, that might sound like a good idea. Selling ignition coils only to gasoline manufacturers *does* sound like a missed opportunity.

But there's a problem with his idea.

In a gasoline engine, the gasoline is injected into the combustion cylinder and combined with air. The compressed air-fuel mixture is ignited by the spark plug. The ignition coil connected to the spark plug transforms the car battery's 12 volts into the thousands of volts necessary to create the spark.

Diesel engines don't do that. Diesel fuel is injected into the combustion cylinder, which contains compressed air. Because the air heats up when compressed, the air ignites the fuel spontaneously. So technically, diesel engines don't use spark plugs and ignition coils.

Ted said Bill was incapable, but Ted hadn't even bothered to ask if what he suggested was possible.

Would it have been a dumb question? Yes. But what's wrong with asking a dumb question? Leaders must stay curious to learn.

Ted would have greatly benefited from asking that innocent question and getting the answer instead of beating Bill up and displaying arrogance.

As a leader, you should know enough about the products and technology in your business to be able to provide sufficient leadership. When you don't know the answer to something—and you won't know the answer to everything—ask the question. Don't be arrogant.

If you treat people as Ted treated Bill, your people won't teach you or correct you when they need to.

Leaders are not expected to know everything. But leaders are expected to know enough that they can ask the right questions. If you are in so far over your head you don't know the basics of the company, your people will lose respect for you. They may not laugh at you. They may say "yes, sir" or "yes, ma'am" in front of you because they are afraid to get fired. But they will laugh at you behind the scenes if you display ignorance and arrogance.

Now imagine at a higher level you didn't understand how the organization worked.

Let's say there was an issue in your monthly operations review, and your behavior makes it clear you don't know how to do your job, you don't know who is doing what, and you don't understand the issues being discussed, even from a 10,000-foot view. If that's the case, you won't know how to fix any issues that come to you.

If you insult the people on the ground who put their blood and sweat into fixing the issue, you will see a negative emergence. When leaders are exposed for having a lack of operational and organizational knowledge, it makes the entire organization go backward. People lose respect for you. Leaders might, for a time, be able to control the situation by wielding their power, but it won't last.

## HOW LEADERS BEGIN TO LEARN WITH TOUGH-LOVE INTERACTIONS

Without the organization, there is no leader. Without a leader, someone else will emerge as the leader.

It's the basics of complexity leadership.

When I was at the Detroit office and I interacted with the sales team, I learned the global program management wasn't working. They were having trouble working well with the people at the Swiss product design center.

I did not know about that conflict before. After I knew about it, I could fix it. Clarity, training, and communication improved the program-management team, and it got back on track. We could then apply those aspects globally. With that fix, the entire program-management process of the company improved.

Leadership is not about micromanaging or running individual projects. It's about discovering the small improvements the organization needs to make, making them, and getting them right at all levels at all times.

In my situation, I still had a knowledge gap. I assumed the projects were running smoothly, but I was wrong. My direct reports had told me that the project was in a good place.

But with the interactions I had, I came to learn that wasn't the case. So, I advised the team on how they could improve cross-cultural communications to launch the project. I had the knowledge and skills necessary to resolve the problem.

I didn't know how the products worked from a deep technical level. I never had to know. That's why we had engineers. It was my job to find the gap and provide direction.

To be capable of finding the gaps, leaders must always be learning. They will always face new issues that have no obvious solutions.

In fact, if you are spending your time resolving obvious issues, your organization isn't working right. Those are things that lower levels of management should be doing. So, fix the process.

Leaders should always be spending time on complex issues dealing with unknown unknowns.

That responsibility requires a great deal of humility. Leaders must be able to admit they don't know everything and ask the right questions. Otherwise, you might find yourself like Ted, asking your team to do something they can't and shouldn't do and feeling stupid for it.

As leaders grapple with the technical knowledge gap, they have the opportunity to model good values and behaviors, as well as set the direction of the company.

But what about aligning the organization toward one common goal, even during uncertain times? That's where organizational knowledge comes in—and leaders must tackle their own organization knowledge gap.

## ORGANIZATION KNOWLEDGE GAP

In 1687, Isaac Newton changed the world by introducing the three laws of motion.[64] These laws state that the speed and the location of an object can be precisely determined using determinism. The idea of determinism further extended to the concept that forces around us, in action long before our lifetimes, set in motion what brought us exactly to where we are today. This theory says we have no real choice and no influence around our circumstances or on the outcome of our efforts.

In 1927, German scientist Werner Heisenberg challenged Isaac Newton's determinism with his uncertainty principle.[65]

According to the Heisenberg uncertainty principle, the position and speed of an object can't be measured at exactly the same time, and also, the concept of exact position and exact speed at the same time has no meaning in real life. Why? Because by the time you find out those exact figures, they're different.

In other words, there is an inherent randomness and complexity in the universe that can't be reduced, even by the likes of Albert Einstein.[66]

If you've made it this far into tackling complexity and uncertainty, this concept is not surprising. It comes back to the fact that the outcomes are not guaranteed based on the decisions we make today.

## HOW LEADERS BEGIN TO LEARN WITH TOUGH-LOVE INTERACTIONS

We've established that we can't even know ourselves perfectly, let alone the enormity about other living and complex things.

But we can take steps to close the gap. The purpose of the interactions we discussed in previous chapters is to learn what we don't know. It's a never-ending process.

It's true for technical knowledge, but it's doubly true when it comes to your team and the organization. Is it emerging positively? Is it aligning with your direction? Is it on the right path? Is it emerging negatively? Is it going against your direction? Is it on the wrong path?

No leader wants to fail. Everyone wants to win and leave behind a victorious legacy.

So then why don't leaders take the right action at the right time?

Because they don't know the truth, whether it be about their own organization, the market, the customers, or the suppliers. If you know the truth, of course you will make the right decision, and you will get things done and be successful.

Remember the purpose of the interaction part of the SIILA model in tackling complexity, which is not to fix individual issues, even though that is often a by-product of your actions. The purpose is to learn the real status of the organization so that you can act early.

When you interact, you will learn these facts quickly:

- Everyone is watching your every move, and you are always sending a message to the organization.
- Your focus should not be on pleasing your boss or shareholders but on being part of the organization.
- You do not have much power yourself. The real power is within the organization itself.
- You never know the truth of what is going on. Even if you learn the truth, by the time you know it, it has already changed.

- Building reputation, establishing credibility, and modeling expected behavior and values are the most powerful weapons you have to lead your organization.

Your great speeches, inspired vision, powerful mission, and the generous benefits you give your employees won't get you very far as a leader if you are unable to interact with your organization and find the truth about it.

How is it possible then, to lead a large organization well? Can you gain the kind of knowledge you need to make it work? Yes, absolutely.

Let's see what we can learn from Larry Culp here.

## GET SMALL THINGS RIGHT

Larry Culp served as the president and CEO of the global science and technology conglomerate Danaher Corporation from 2000 to 2014. During this time, sales grew fivefold to $20 billion, and the market capitalization grew from $10 billion to $50 billion.[67] Danaher Business System (DBS) is the engine behind this success. In the mid-1980s, the company launched the system, an effort based on the ideas around lean manufacturing, that it widely credits with driving a consistent cycle of change and improvement.[68]

The process aims to have exceptional people developing outstanding plans, to execute the plans using world-class tools, and to construct sustainable processes resulting in superior performance.

The fundamental core behind DBS is the application of the *go-see* approach of Japanese manufacturing philosophy that involves *genba* (where the action is), *kaizen* (continuous improvement), *andon* (notification to management of any issues), and *kanban* (visual monitoring).

This overarching concept covers everything from engineering, to finance, to HR, to the supply chain. After all, it's all about the mindset and common sense.

It's also all about the interactions with the go-see approach. It brings visibility to issues that may not otherwise be brought to management until it's too late. It's about getting the little things done right, and it's about always looking for ways to do better. It's a continuous cycle.

The DBS is common sense. There's nothing magical about it, just as there is nothing magical about the Toyota Production System. The whole system is available for anyone to learn and copy. But to pull it off, the leader has to create the mindset. It can't be done by LED display boards, new presentation formats, terminologies, or hiring consultants.

Larry Culp mastered it and internalized it. He believed in these principles. To tackle complexity, leaders must have the right interactions at all levels.

Culp went on to teach these fundamentals at Harvard Business School after he retired from Danaher in 2014.

Once the leader is focused on getting these small things done right and demonstrates the appropriate behavior, the organization follows. Before you know it, the positive emergence is throughout the organization, regardless of how large it is.

Here is another example to demonstrate how the right behavior cascades down in the organization.

I once took my executive team for an off-site meeting and started to reflect on how we were doing as a team to identify areas of improvement. Before the workshop, I sent everyone two leadership books and gave them a few questions to lead our discussions.

The whole team got a lot out of that simple exercise.

Weeks later, I learned all the executives took what we did in those sessions and replicated it with the rest of their staff. I didn't ask them to do that, but I was happy they did. When I asked my executives to read those books and engaged with them deeply on the subject material, it set an example. They saw I wasn't just distributing books to show off. We were deeply engaged with the discussions. They saw real value in the exercise.

Similarly, if you say one thing but do another, you are sending a message that what you say is not important. It says you cannot be trusted. You will see negative emergence with this behavior, and by then it's too late.

## TACKLING COMPLEXITY

These learnings are key for leaders to improve themselves.

Imagine if Dennis Muilenburg, the former CEO of Boeing, knew his people misunderstood his cost-reduction initiative? Imagine if he knew they were taking risks that were simply too high. But therein lay his knowledge gap.

In part II (the chapters on systems thinking), we discussed how everything is interconnected and how complex systems emerge.

In Muilenburg's case, the organization emerged negatively.

If he did not know that, why didn't he know what was going on?

Because he did not learn. Why? *Because he did not interact.*

Even after the plane crashes, he did not *go see* the crash sites, and his interactions with regulators, customers, and the public were subpar. Those mistakes cost Boeing CEO Dennis Muilenburg his job.[69]

His inaction demonstrates the power of a leader's inability to interact with all levels of the internal organization as well as with outside stakeholders.

The way you keep learning is to keep interacting. You must have your antennae up. Have a system in which issues get escalated to you. These are great opportunities for us to learn.

Remember that Alan Mullaly, the man who went from Boeing to Ford, was not a Detroit automotive executive. He was an aerospace engineer and aircraft expert. He had a technical knowledge gap and an organization knowledge gap—but he knew that, and he did something about it. He interacted with all levels and connected with global teams so that he could fill in his technical and organizational knowledge gaps.

Good "people leaders" are hard to find.

In the next chapter, we'll talk about how leaders teach to learn and why great leaders are great teachers.

# CHAPTER 11

# YOUR LEADERSHIP IS TESTED ON THIS ONE STEP

We've all heard the saying "Give a man a fish and you feed him for a day. Teach a man to fish and you feed him for a lifetime."

How does this look in business environments?

Great leaders love working with people. If a man comes to them and asks for food (or help with a big problem), a great leader will teach that man how to fish (or fix the problem), so that man will never come back needing help with the same problem.

If he *does* come back, the leader either didn't teach him well the first time, or the guy is just lazy.

Teaching is one of the best ways leaders can learn about their people, the organization, and themselves.

Consciously or unconsciously, leaders are always teaching those around them. With every step they take, they are sending messages to the organization. If a leader understands their effect, they can use it to transform organizations positively.

Leaders practice many active ways of teaching too. They could be simply teaching something during a regular meeting or interaction, using issues that come up as learning opportunities, or teaching in a regular classroom. Great leaders who understand the power of teaching to learn do all those things.

Successful leaders in complexity are willing to give their team members hands-on training instead of just simply ordering them around and expecting them to be followers.

General Electric CEO Jack Welch popularized the concept of leader as teacher. Jack Welch not only gave the welcome speech at the Crotonville Leadership Institute of GE; he was also a regular teacher in the program. He invested many hours personally developing the next generation of leaders.[70]

When a leader is focused on developing people, cultivating their desires to learn and stretch, individuals have the chance to rise and unleash their true potential. Such attention brings out the best in people and helps them achieve their own personal goals, which means the organization does better too.

The CEO of PepsiCo, Roger Enrico, started and led a program called Executive Leadership: Building the Business. He spent five days fully engaged, teaching, and he held a 90-day follow-up where participants applied what they learned and got coaching from Enrico himself. At the end of the 90 days, there was a three-day session for everyone to share what they learned. Through his teaching program, Enrico unearthed the next CEO of PepsiCo, Indra Nooyi.[71]

YOUR LEADERSHIP IS TESTED ON THIS ONE STEP

## THE POWER OF TEACHING TO LEARN AND INFLUENCE

Leaders leave their legacies for others to follow and grow. They do it by teaching. When the teaching stops, the learning stops. At that point, growth stops, and the organization begins to decline.

Some leaders may be afraid to get out in front of their people. Some may question why the leader needs to teach at all. Didn't they hire the best people? Others may say leaders are too busy doing other things and don't have time to teach.

Leaders, through continual learning and teaching, build the foundation of the organization. Just as thousands of years ago the teachings of Socrates, Plato, Aristotle, Sun Tzu, and others helped build the civilization that we embrace today, modern-day leaders have more power and influence than anyone else in your organization to build the foundation with the right culture and behavior that everyone must embrace.

One of the reasons Welch and Enrico taught so much was because they learned much more about their organizations while teaching than they did during normal business reviews. They also learned a lot about their employees, from their struggles to their mindsets, which enabled them to devise appropriate interventions and strategies for their businesses.

For the leader, the biggest benefit of teaching is the learning that comes with it. Remember this part of the SIILA model is about learning. The leader has to teach to learn.

When a leader teaches, he will know if the concepts, skills, values, and behaviors that he is using are moving the organization in the right direction.

If they are not, leaders must make necessary adjustments in order to create positive emergence of the organization.

Teaching also helps build trust. It gives participants a chance to get close to the leader, seeing firsthand how the leader aligns themselves to the values of the organization and models good behavior. Such knowledge helps people grow and develop into the best versions of themselves for themselves, which ultimately helps the organization achieve its goals and get things done.

Leaders are always looking for people with potential and trying to place them in the right jobs. Teaching is a great way to get to know your people and build a strong talent pipeline with key positions, or for succession planning. That way, when you need to fill a position, you don't have to panic and just bring in an unknown from the outside. You'll likely already have someone in mind to fill the role.

When you don't know the capabilities and skills of the people within the organization, you have to bring in people from outside. As we discussed earlier, no amount of interviews can really tell how good or bad the person you hire is. Such insight can take years to perceive, and by the time you know, it could be too late. At the same time, if you hire someone from outside while there is talent within the company, good people will quit. They lose trust in the senior leaders.

We spoke about Boeing and Ford earlier in previous chapters. It's interesting how Boeing struggled, and Alan Mulally, who came from Boeing, saved Ford.

Alan Mulally was the president and CEO of Boeing Commercial Airplanes when Harry Stonecipher was the CEO of Boeing. In 2005, Stonecipher was forced to resign from Boeing following the disclosure of an affair with a subordinate, in violation of the Boeing code of conduct.

Many thought Mulally's success in the commercial airplanes group and his decades of loyal service would have earned him the CEO spot of Boeing. But after Stonecipher departed, the top post went instead to James McNerney, chief executive of 3M, a multinational manufacturing conglomerate—in other words, an outsider.[72] Mulally left Boeing and became the CEO of Ford and did really well.[73]

It's so important for leaders to know their people. People decisions cannot be delegated. A leader must be deeply involved. Teaching is a great way for leaders to know their people.

## YOUR LEADERSHIP IS TESTED ON THIS ONE STEP

A leader who is involved on the ground level and teaching employees how to become better people and do their jobs also has the opportunity to share the bigger picture with people across the organization. In this moment, leaders have the power to explain and demonstrate why it's important to do certain things in certain ways, which helps people to connect the dots and work to achieve bigger organizational goals.

We all know that we need more leaders to achieve our aspirations. The best way to create more leaders is by having today's leaders nurturing tomorrow's leaders.

Beyond the benefits that leaders are sure to reap in the future, teaching also helps them to master their own domain. The more they teach, the deeper their expertise. As they teach, they become better leaders.

In short, when a leader teaches, it creates a kind of feedback loop. People in the organization learn from the leader, and the leader learns from them. At that point, the leader can take action to change himself and the organization to get things done while delivering performance and tackling complexity.

If teaching is so powerful for a complexity leader, how can a leader go about teaching?

We discussed that teaching can take place at anytime and anywhere. For good teaching to happen, leaders must have a point of view about what they teach and leadership.

## WHAT IS TEACHABLE POINT OF VIEW?

People are always looking for ways to win and to work better with the people around them. Both are as true at work as in our personal lives. That's why there are so many books, talks, social media content, and formal classes where people are looking for knowledge and inspiration to work toward whatever goal they have in life.

Every time I visit one of our remote sites, I do regular operations reviews, plant walk-throughs, town halls, and other leadership events. But

I always take it a step further. I always make sure that I spend at least 90 minutes with young employees. During this time, no managers are allowed to be around.

These young employees just started their careers. They have a lot to learn, and they are hungry to learn it. But I have a lot to learn from them too. I meet these people to help them in any possible way as they start life, to align with the long-term goals of the company, and to learn the pulse of the young talent. They are our future.

When I have these meetings, I always make a point to crack a joke and put everyone at ease. I've found that unless you can cross that line and make your audience feel comfortable and relaxed, they won't trust you enough to talk with you about what's really on their minds.

I once visited a manufacturing plant and held one of these young-talent interactions. After a long day of formal meetings, these are always my favorite.

I asked a simple question: "Why do you want to grow in your career?"

There were 20 young employees in the room that day. One of the answers touched me, and I can remember it to this day.

A female employee in her early 20s spoke up. She explained that when her mother got pregnant, her lover left her and her unborn baby. Her mother decided to keep the baby—her—and go through all the pains of the social and physical sacrifices to be a single mother.

"I am that baby," she said. "Nothing is more important to me than making my mother's decision worth it by making her proud of who I am."

She had tears in her eyes, and so did I.

There were other great answers too, like "want to prove myself," "contribute," "help others," "be a good role model to my children" and many more. But her aspiration hit home.

It struck me, and always does, that their goals did not revolve around how fast they could get a convertible sports car or buy a beachfront property. They didn't have ambitions to be the richest person in the class or the community.

I'm sure money motivated many of them to some degree, but they all had deep feelings and real goals beyond that.

The more leaders can see the people who work for them as human beings with complex lives, the more successful we will be. It's our job to help our people achieve their goals as they grow within our company.

So, I asked the room full of young talent to write down their answer to my question. I told them to keep it safe, looking at that answer again at least once a month. I advised them not to chase money, power, or social status, as those things will be taken away when all of us one day get old, sick, and die.

More importantly, I told them they shouldn't wait until they were in their 70s to enjoy their lives and find meaning in them. All of it should be integrated into life.

They loved that speech. No one expected something so personal from the president. They thought I'd come in and tell them to work hard, deliver more, and compete with the best. Do you really think these young people, who just started working for you, care about the company before you have a chance to establish yourself as a trustworthy leader who understands their hopes and dreams and will help them achieve their goals? They can easily find another job, and they will if you only talk about the business and what it needs from them.

Many leaders out there say millennials and Gen Y are difficult to work with. I think it's totally the opposite. They are smarter, and they know a hundred times more than we knew at their age. The issue is that older generations have a hard time connecting with them. Of course, seniors have more experience and have seen more life—but that doesn't mean they're right about everything. Younger generations will challenge you, and that's a good thing. Together, we can work through what to accept—old and new.

Ultimately, it's important to let your people, especially your young people, know that it's okay if it takes them time to figure out what they want out of life. Make it clear you will help them figure it out.

Some find out who they are and what they want in life early enough, and some don't.

## BE HERE NOW

Let's look at the journey that some leaders took to find out who they are.

Ram Dass, a Harvard professor, spiritual leader, and author of the book *Be Here Now,* is largely credited for introducing Eastern concepts such as meditation, mindfulness, and the practice of yoga to American culture. He is particularly well known for inspiring leaders like Steve Jobs.

He has his own story too.

Richard Alpert was born to a wealthy family in Newton, Massachusetts. His father was the founder of Brandeis University and president of the New Haven Railroad. Alpert got his PhD in psychology from Stanford University and was hired as a professor at Harvard University.[74]

While at Harvard, he started a personal research project in which he began taking hallucinogenic drugs. Harvard, of course, didn't condone this, and it eventually got him fired. Suddenly, he found himself with a lot of free time.

During that time, Alpert decided to travel to India as a tourist. There he met an American turned spiritual wanderer, Bhagavan Das, who began to teach him mindfulness. The timing was impeccable, as Alpert, struggling with the loss of his job, couldn't stop thinking about the past and worried constantly about what the future would bring.

Whenever Alpert started to talk about his past, Bhagavan Das would say, "Don't think about the past. Just be here now."

Whenever Alpert asked a question about where they were going and what the future would hold, Bhagavan Das would say, "Don't think about the future. Just be here now."

Eventually, Bhagavan Das brought Alpert to guru Neem Karoli Baba, also known as *Maharaj-ji* (the great king), and Alpert learned yoga, meditation, and mindfulness at a deep emotional level. Richard Alpert was then given the name Ram Dass, and he learned to reach enlightenment and find the meaning of life through meditation. In the past, he'd only been able to find that feeling with psychedelics.

In 1968, he returned to the U.S., now a bushy-bearded, barefoot, white-robed guru. Following his return, he got a nationwide radio show in which he shared his experience with Maharaja-ji.

"When I'm in his presence I experience ecstasy and bliss from the depth of the love that our relationship has for me, and that's a drunken kind of love where I often find myself just dissolved into tears because I've just never experienced such profound love from any being."[75]

This quote sums up well what kind of impression a quality teacher can, and I would say, should make. All leaders are teachers. All leaders have a story. We have to tell our story to connect with people to unleash that potential everyone has but may be guarding because they don't yet know who they are.

Everyone is looking for inspiration and to find out who they are.

How does this search work in leadership?

Steve Jobs was the founder and CEO of Apple. He helped to revolutionize the computer, music, and mobile communication industries. Jobs was born to unmarried graduate students and was adopted as a baby by a Silicon Valley machinist and his wife.

As a teenager, while attending Reed College, Steve Jobs read Ram Dass's book, *Be Here Now*. He found the book hugely influential, and he took up meditation.[76]

The book inspired Jobs to travel to India to meet Maharaj-ji. But his journey was very different from the one Ram Dass experienced. How could it not be? A trip to India will be experienced very differently by a penniless, teenage college dropout than it would be for an ex-Harvard professor from a rich family.[77]

Nevertheless, Jobs swapped out his jeans and T-shirts for lungis and began his journey from New Delhi to the Himalayas.

Every Sunday, Jobs walked seven miles to get a free meal at the Hare Krishna temple. Jobs slept in abandoned buildings and survived on local food.

Sometimes, things got desperate.

One day, while sleeping in a dry creek bed, Jobs and his friend Dan Kottke were trapped in a fierce thunderstorm. Kottke later told that they prayed to any god who could hear them in that moment. "Dear God, if I ever get through this, I'll be a good person, I promise."

Despite all he went through during his journey, Jobs never got to meet guru Maharaj-ji. He died before Jobs could meet him.

So, what did Jobs learn from his journey?

Jobs found that India was far poorer than he had imagined. He was struck by the incongruity between the country's condition and its airs of holiness. He wanted to contribute to the world in a different way.

The India trip did not help Jobs meet Maharaj-ji or find his way of enlightenment. But he found another truth and another path. The trip marked a turning point in his life.

In his own words, the India trip helped him realize that "Thomas Edison did a lot more to improve the world than Karl Marx and Neem Karoli Baba put together."[78]

Thomas Edison was driven with a goal to make technology cheaper for the masses, while other inventors of the time focused on luxury and industrial customers. Edison worked to come up with mechanical and electrical designs to make reliable, mass-producible products and thus created General Electric in 1890.

Steve Jobs founded Apple and built one of the greatest companies on Earth. He was always honest about his story and shared it with his people. His candor helped to create one of the most innovative company cultures in the world.

Jobs maintained that spirituality. Even after he became ill with cancer, he went to India to continue meditation.[79]

Though neither Edison nor Jobs was perfect (who among us is?), their contributions to our lives are undeniable.

The point here is that leaders tell their own stories to help teach people how to win. Their openness helps get things done. But in order to teach, you must have a teachable point of view.

## WHAT IS YOUR TEACHABLE POINT OF VIEW?

The best teachable point of view is your own story.

Professor Noel Tichy, who once led the General Electric Leadership Center, came up with the idea that leaders must have a teachable point of view. A teachable point of view is a leader's opinion on what it takes to win in his or her business and what it takes to lead other people.

All leaders must have an opinion on what it takes to win in business and lead other people. But the real question is this: is your point of view on how to win in business and lead others teachable?

Simply put, your ideas must be accepted by your students—in this case, your employees. If the values and behavior you teach aren't accepted by others, if it goes against their own values and behavior in irreconcilable ways, how can you possibly align the organization and get things done?

Isn't it "get down to managing yourself" that we internalized earlier in the book? Here is another real-life example on how powerful the teachable point of view is when the leader knows it.

## YOU, YOUR JOB, AND YOUR CAREER

Recently, I was invited to give a one-hour training at a project-management conference. One might think I would have taught attendees how to keep schedules, make timelines, and follow up in order to launch projects on time with the right cost and quality.

But there were plenty of speakers after me who could teach about those technicalities.

I wrote on a flip chart that I would speak about three things: you, your job, and your career.

I told a story about a leader who was always late for meetings. Subsequently, his subordinates also started showing up late. He learned that it was his behavior causing subordinates to be late, so he forced himself to be punctual at work. But he was still extremely unreliable with commitments in his personal life. For example, he promised his grandma he would go visit her for lunch during the weekend, but he arrived six hours late. His poor grandma prepared food with a lot of love, but she found herself waiting around all day.

People can't act one way in one place and another way in a different place. The hardest thing to do is manage yourself, but if you manage yourself consistently and you do it well, your life and career will naturally be successful.

Then I asked the group what they noticed as symptoms of someone who can't manage themselves. They had great answers.

- They blame others when things go wrong.
- They make a lot of excuses.
- They feel as if they are unlucky.
- They feel they are never wrong.
- They feel the world is not fair to them.

These are not my answers. These are the answers from the 50 project managers who attended the conference.

Now think of how powerful this message is in promoting an accountability culture. If project managers hold themselves accountable for launching projects on time, they will spot risk earlier and ask for help when they need it.

That correlation means projects get finished. It means employees are happy as they learn and grow and build a strong career. They become happy at work *and* in their life.

## YOUR LEADERSHIP IS TESTED ON THIS ONE STEP

I often tell my managers they must be reinventing themselves to find a better version of themselves—and I really mean it. If these project managers become great managers, who benefits the most?

Frankly, they do. They become better people in life and better managers at work. If for some reason they have to find another job, they will always be successful because they are great project managers. Their life will be peaceful.

I once sent 200 of my managers to a business school for their own growth. I didn't sign a bond or additional contract with those managers stating that they had to remain with the company for a certain amount of time. The university was surprised by that freedom. University staff told me they had never seen such a policy, as companies usually have employees sign some sort of contract if they sponsor education.

My focus is teaching my managers to become better managers and better people for themselves. Of course, once they make those kinds of improvements, they may find jobs elsewhere. That's when real leadership gets tested.

I want to do everything I can to equip my people to do their best. I want them to work for me, not because of a contract but because they trust my leadership and want to work for me despite tempting opportunities. Leaders must be willing to build that kind of trust-based bond with their people rather than seek security from a piece of paper.

I strongly believe in that strategy, and it's how I choose to manage. I learned how it all works thanks to experience—the hardest teacher of all. But it works.

So, leaders must have a teachable point of view. They must have the chance to teach it and test if it works.

Acquiring a teachable point of view requires in-depth preparation, reflection on your past success and failures, and revelation about who you are and what is important to and for you. Once a leader has a teachable point of view, they can teach in all kinds of creative ways. They can—and should—turn every interaction with their people into a learning and teaching event. They don't complain that there is no time; instead, they often set aside time to teach.

When leaders start sharing where they come from, what they believe in, what they expect from the team, and what the team should expect from their leaders, clarity is established and trust is built with people.

This trust leads to better alignment and motivation for the organization to emerge positively, which increases performance and gets things done.

If leaders find that what they're teaching isn't working, it's a sign there is a problem with their point of view and their leadership itself. It is an opportunity for leaders to learn and adjust.

# PART V REVIEW

In part V, we discussed the learning part of the SIILA model in tackling complexity. Here are the key takeaways:

- In tackling complexity, learning is the most important skill that leaders must develop. Every other skill will become obsolete over time, but the skill of learning will serve you for however long you use it.
- Leaders must always seek to learn technical knowledge on the product, services, processes, policies, governance, etc. and to work to close the organizational knowledge gap on people and culture.
- People are always looking for ways to win and to work better. That premise is a great opportunity for leaders to share their teachable point of view and leadership point of view to align the organization with good values and to create positive outcomes.

Learning is great—but unless leaders apply what they've learned and are willing to change because of it, that learning is useless. In the next part of the book, we will talk about the last step in the SIILA model, which is adapt.

# PART VI

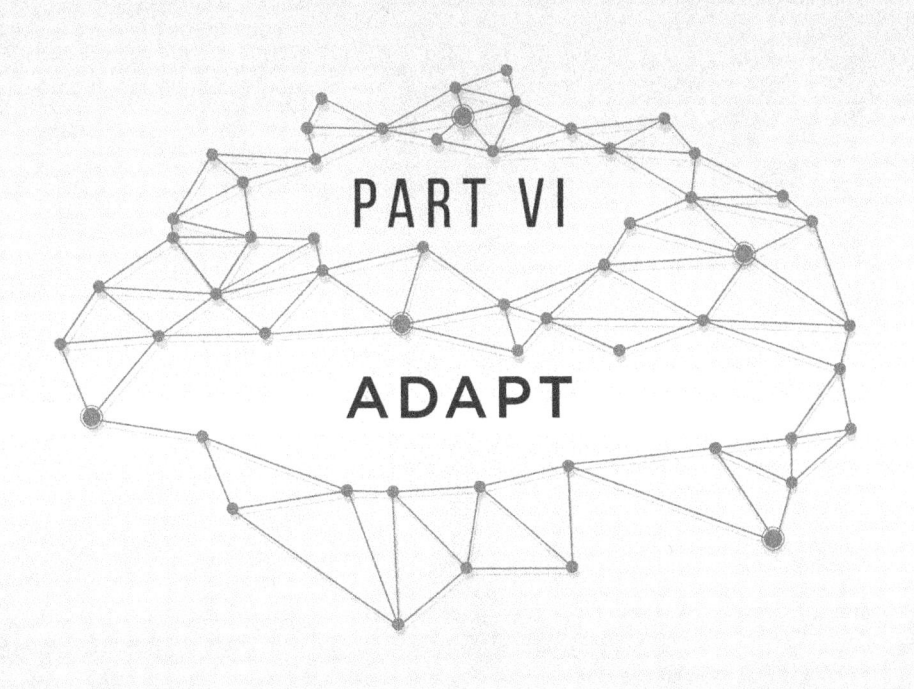

# ADAPT

# CHAPTER 12

# IT'S NOT THE KNOWLEDGE…
# IT'S WHAT YOU DO WITH IT

A friend of mine once told me her relationship with her teenage son wasn't good. After a number of fights and misunderstandings, they both felt the other didn't care about each other. So, she read a book that promised she would learn how to improve her relationship with her son. But it didn't help. So, she read another book; it still didn't help. She told me all the books were great—they had great stories, ideas, and advice on how parents can improve relationships with their children. She read more than 10 books, but she still wasn't making any progress with her son.

I told her to stop reading books. She knew what the problem was, just as she knew the solution. I am sure the first book told her everything she needed to know—she just hadn't taken any action to make it happen. The first book already told her she needed to start accepting that the boy was growing into his own as an adult, to stop focusing on his weaknesses, and to begin having an open discussion about the relationship with him.

But the learning itself had no value if she could not change herself.

That's why reading too many books won't help you. You need to start practicing what's in the books. Reading an abundance of books may help you sound smart. It may even help you get a job. But to get things done, you must execute what you've learned.

In the previous chapter we talked about the time when I sent 200 of my managers to a business school. The program they attended consisted of all the hard and soft skills you might learn in an MBA program. All the managers had bachelor's degrees, some even had their masters' or doctorates.

After the session, I asked what they learned. The answers were consistent:

- What I knew before is no longer valid, and I have to continue to learn.
- There is so much that I don't know.
- My fellow managers are so much smarter than I thought.

That was an "aha moment" for the team. The money, time, and effort put into creating and designing the program paid off. These were all great lessons.

But now imagine that all 200 managers changed their behavior based on what they learned. Imagine they continued to value humility, sought to learn more, and began unleashing others' true potential. What kind of performance could we then achieve in our organization?

Focusing on having better managers and a thriving organization will help you to build a strong culture. The effort will naturally position you to have better products and services than the competition.

But will the leaders change? After the warm memories of the training session is over, after the excitement wears off, will they return to old habits?

As we discussed in previous chapters, leaders must interact to learn what they don't know. Then they know what they don't know. But learning is useless if you cannot change. This is the last step in the SIILA model: leaders must adapt.

Leaders today talk a lot about how difficult it is to change their organizations. And it's true that it is difficult.

One survey conducted by McKinsey & Company found the failure rate of organizational transformations to be higher than 60%, while a *Harvard Business Review* study suggested more than 70% of transformation efforts fail.[80]

Leaders use a lot of resources to make transformations perfect, from hiring experts, to starting training programs, to making timelines, and more. So, why do they still fail to change their organizations?

A leader will never change their organization until they change themselves. Leaders must start by changing themselves to ensure the success of organizational change.

I once promoted a new general manager to lead a business unit. He was incredibly intelligent and had all the higher education and background necessary for the job. During his first 60 days on the job, he noticed the team's decision-making skills seemed to get weaker. He started making changes, working to coach and train his team to help them improve.

For a while, he would come to me and talk about the problems he had with his sales director. He talked about several options for the sales director, including putting him in another job, having another sales director take on half his workload, firing him, and even promoting him. It seemed like every day he had a new idea for the sales director.

It was then I realized his problem. He couldn't make decisions. He spent so much time trying to correct behavior in his team that he didn't realize their behavior came from him.

In my coaching with him, I told him he needed to realize his organization wouldn't improve or mature until he could change himself and work on his own shortcomings. He was a smart guy. He listened to my feedback, recognized his problem, lost a few nights of sleep, and came back stronger.

Acknowledging that fact isn't a new challenge for leaders. In fact, it's a centuries-old problem. The famous Russian novelist Leo Tolstoy even wrote, "Everyone thinks of changing the world, but no one thinks of changing himself."[81]

In tackling complexity to get things done, the last action leaders must take is to adapt in order to deliver results. When leaders combine systems thinking, internalize the right mindset, interact with the stakeholders, learn what they don't know, *and* adapt what they've learned, they will get the results they're after. That is the SIILA model.

So, leaders must change themselves based on what they've learned. Knowing is not enough. They must take real action and make real change.

Why is this part so difficult? It takes regular, conscious effort.

Think of the last time you went to the doctor for your annual health checkup. Maybe your doctor tells you to exercise and watch your diet to lose 20 pounds of weight to keep your heart healthy. Of course, it wouldn't hurt that losing a couple of pounds would make you feel more comfortable and look more attractive.

Maybe you buy a treadmill or sign up for a gym membership. But how many people continue with regular exercise and a healthy diet to achieve that goal?

It's easier to stick to your old habits. There will always be resistance to change. When people say they are too busy or they don't have time to make those changes, that's only the tip of the iceberg.

## WHY CAN'T LEADERS CHANGE THEMSELVES?

A leader must understand their own resistance and make a commitment to confront that resistance to change in order to move forward.

What happens when leaders can't, or won't, change?

## IT'S NOT THE KNOWLEDGE... IT'S WHAT YOU DO WITH IT

In complexity, everything around us is changing. Leaders can't stand still *and* make progress happen. If leaders don't continually change themselves and adapt, the leader and the organization are moving backward.

Let's take a real-life example from business.

I once worked for a business that saw exponential growth for 15 years. The revenue grew more than tenfold during this period as markets exploded and the company capitalized on it.

However, markets eventually started slowing down, becoming more mature markets with slower growth. More competitors entered the market, and customers demanded lower prices and improved product quality. Good employees had more job opportunities outside and left the company.

The financial performance of the business was deteriorating. Quality and delivery issues exploded, worsened by a labor strike as the company relocated a manufacturing plant from one location to a less expensive location just 100 kilometers away. The strike alone cost the company $20 million.

As a result, my predecessor stepped down, and I took over.

My first impression of the business was a visceral one. It reminded me of a pond when the water level was high—you could only see the beautiful scenery. But when the water level went down, you started to see crocodiles and other dangers lurking just beneath the surface. At the company, many performance issues were below the surface, obscured as the company brought in revenue and profit. They didn't just appear one day; they were always there.

Leaders can be blinded by good financial performance in a company if they don't understand why the performance is good and how the results are delivered. This kind of knowledge gap is the perfect path to failure when the good times are over. It made turning around the company very difficult, especially for a team that only saw growth in the past.

Typically, when I see a manufacturing plant experiencing major issues, I would immediately go to the plant myself and bring the operations director with me. If the issues were big, I'd stay a few days until I felt comfortable with understanding the issues and have the operations director stay longer to help sort things out and bring back normalcy. This go-see culture helps me make leaders accountable and resolve issues faster when they are small.

We once encountered a plant manager who was having major performance and behavior issues. We had to let him go—but the operations director refused to see him and inform him of the decision. Instead, he chose to stay out of the process entirely, even though the plant manager was his direct report. In a meeting with another senior executive, this operations director told us that he had never fired anyone in his career.

The other executive looked at me and asked, "How could someone become an operations director and run a very large organization without ever having to fire someone?"

Later, I came to learn that whenever there was a bad performer working under this operations director, the poor performer was moved to a different, easier task, and another person would do the job. This is okay to do one or two times. After all, one poor performance doesn't make someone a bad employee—but if you make it a habit, you end up keeping all the poor performers and making other people do the work. The outcome is that the people cost doubles, and the organizational culture goes backward.

High revenue can cover these extra costs and inefficiencies for a time, but when revenue falls, the real fundamental problems of a business start to surface.

This director said all the right things about needing to change, firing poor performers, being accountable, improving profitability, etc., but he was never able to face reality and change himself.

It was painful to watch. In the past, he was one of the best performers in the company. But he could not change himself. He knew how to manage the growth of the business but couldn't navigate the turnaround of the business. If he had been able to change himself and adapt to the new realities of the business, he would have been my successor. But he couldn't—and eventually he resigned as the pressure continued to build and he felt as if he was losing himself.

But there were many other leaders in the company who could accept that change and develop their careers to become strong leaders, even in turnaround times.

You can ask others to change, but unless you can change yourself, it doesn't matter. That measure is how you can tell if a leader has truly internalized what it means to be a leader.

## WHY IS CHANGE SO HARD?

The work here begins deep inside yourself. Others can show you the path to take, but you have to take those baby steps to move forward and challenge your own inner resistance.

There could be many reasons why leaders don't change themselves, even after they know what they need to do. Although there could be very many factors, the following are some of the common reasons why leaders don't change:[82]

- worry about the risks of the change—it feels easier and safer to stay with the devil they know;
- fear of losing who they are now—the feeling that it always worked in the past;
- feeling stressed over the existing workload and issues to resolve;
- feeling unloved and unsupported from rest of the organization, making the leader protect himself;
- anger with themselves, and emotions take the lead;
- an inability to see a path forward; or
- a lack of urgency to change; therefore, they procrastinate.[83]

Leaders are humans. They have all the feelings everyone else does. Whatever the cause of your resistance, it blocks your change and prevents you from moving forward.

As a first step in combating this resistance, it's important to identify your own self-change profile.

## INDIVIDUAL CHANGE PROFILE

In previous chapters, we talked about the importance of knowing yourself and why that requirement is a lifelong journey. We know the process never ends because we all keep changing, and that's complexity. So, you must find out what prevents you from changing even after you know what you have to change.

Change is personal.

Once I had a career discussion with a young sales manager. At the time, he was 34 years old. I asked him about his career ambition, and he had no answer. I got very specific with him and asked, "What job do you want to have when you are 45 years old?"

He hesitated for a moment before saying, "I want to be a good person."

That's a great life goal, but this was a career-planning discussion. I pressed him hard for an answer. When he still couldn't come up with one, I asked him to come back in a week and tell me.

After struggling to speak up, he finally got the words out.

"I want to be a general manager of a business," he said.

Now that's an answer!

Later I asked him why it was so difficult for him to say that in the first place. I was curious.

"I knew the answer," he said, "but I was worried that the others would get the impression I wasn't stable at my current job and was too ambitious for growth."

So, he was hesitant to speak up because he didn't want to tarnish the image he had in his current role.

As a leader, you have to have the courage to speak the truth. He changed, and later he became a general manager.

Let's look at another example.

## IT'S NOT THE KNOWLEDGE... IT'S WHAT YOU DO WITH IT

When a communications manager left the company, we asked a female employee who worked under the previous manager to take on the job. She did a great job except for the fact she refused to do any public speaking. She refused to even introduce the agenda during town hall meetings or make presentations to small groups.

She had no confidence in her public speaking skills and worried everyone would laugh at her mistakes. So, her insecurities were her resistance to change.

It would have been easy to let her go or hire someone from outside for the spot, but because of the quality of her previous work, we kept her in the job. She had no choice but to practice. And she did. She practiced at home in front of the mirror. She practiced presenting at home to family and friends. She worked hard to build her confidence and improve her skills, and she became a successful communications manager and public speaker.

Everyone has their own profile. Discovering what prevents you from changing is critical to overcoming your own resistance and making change happen.

Your individual change profile is a combination of habits, values, beliefs, emotions, hopes, and behavior in various circumstances. Finding how to describe your own common internal tendencies that drive behavior is a good start. Successful leaders continually develop their own change profile to be broader and deeper so that they can continue to overcome resistance and deploy the best path to change themselves.

In the examples we discussed, fear (of losing image) and insecurity (with public speaking) prevented change. In those examples, the managers were able to overcome their resistance to change. But what happens when they encounter another resistance?

The hard work doesn't end when you overcome one problem. Change is a continual process.

Much like internalizing, overcoming resistance is your own task. You may seek help and get it—but eventually you will have to make it happen. At the end of the day, leaders must be committed to tackling complexity to get things done to deliver on expectations. So, successful leaders must be willing and able to change themselves. They must be willing to adapt. This is not an option.

In the next chapter, we will talk about how leaders can make change a habit and how organizations transform when leaders change themselves.

# CHAPTER 13

# REINVENTING BETTER VERSIONS

The accountability and the purpose of leadership is clear from the systems thinking and initialization. So, to get things done, motivated by this accountability and purpose, leaders interact inside and outside the organization to learn. They fill in technical knowledge as well as the organizational knowledge gaps.

To recap from the last chapter, for leaders to adapt they

- identify the knowledge gap,
- acquire the necessary knowledge,
- identify the individual change profile to develop a personal change plan, and
- make an unwavering commitment to change and adapt.

There are plenty of personal advisers, self-help books, psychological advice, templates, and even software tools available to manage a change. But, when it comes to self-change, there will always be help for you if you are willing to listen and learn about what you don't know and to acquire knowledge for it.

The next part of identifying the self-change profile is developing a plan to change and committing to it. Others can't help you with this.

For the change to stick, you need to commit to the change until it becomes a habit that is integrated into your value system.

Remember the leader who was constantly running late for meetings? His subordinates were left waiting, and eventually they started to show up to the meetings late too. Thanks to some interactions this leader had within the organization, he realized that by not being punctual, he was creating a bad example. He was creating a culture in which people did not care about being on time.

The leader identified the problem and adapted to be punctual. He started to come to meetings on time since then.

But what did the change look like throughout the rest of his life?

He promised his grandma he would visit her at lunch during the weekend. He arrived six hours late, even though his grandma prepared a nice lunch for him with lots of love and waited for him.

As grandmas tend to do, she may have told him she understood he is busy. Maybe he got away without a lecture. But think of his tendency from the standpoint of his habits as a leader.

At work, he adapted to be punctual. But was this really true? No. He was on time at work out of fear. His real self had not changed. It was only a matter of time before he fell back into old habits.

To truly change and adapt, remember the internalize part of the SIILA model: for a change to become a habit, successful leaders must internalize it.

Think of a leader who shouts and yells during meetings, doesn't let others speak up, and acts as if he is the smartest person in the room. Such behavior will result in his not knowing the truth about the company. People will be unhappy, and they will leave. Eventually, he will not be able to get things done.

Let's say he goes to a school focused on manners and learns how to behave and how to show people respect. If he is only learning how to look as if he can do those things, how long do you think he will be on his best behavior?

So, the real power is in a leader's mind. A leader must internalize the change and make it an unconscious, stress-free habit.

As the old saying goes, change is the only constant. Leaders who make change a habit transform organizations to continuously win.

## REINVENTING YOURSELF

In early 2000, I was a technical lead for automotive engine electronics controls in Delphi, Singapore. My job was to make sure we had a good new product line ready before customers asked for it. I worked with semiconductor companies such as Infineon and Freescale to define next-generation integrated circuits, which took about three years to develop. After that, we designed engine controllers with other devices and software. Getting everything validated with customers would take another two or three years. So, we had to get these products defined at least five years before introducing them to the market.

At the time, we had a competitive assessment center where we spent time tearing down competitors' products to ensure ours were superior by the time we launched them.

I learned that there is a fundamental flaw in this approach.

Product development took five years in our R&D labs. We did competitive assessments by tearing down our competitors' current products already on the market. We had no idea what our competitors were working on in their R&D labs.

There was a big chance that by the time we launched our products, our competitors had better products than we did, because we were competing with our competitors' old products.

So, I had to change it.

We started challenging ourselves to be our best. We set aggressive targets for ourselves. Instead of trying to follow someone else, we tried to be

## TACKLING COMPLEXITY

the best we could. After all, if we are the market leader, there's no one we can follow. We can only keep reinventing ourselves to be better.

When I shared the new concept, Managing Director Jimmy Quah told me a story.

He and some other senior managers from different companies were invited to a take a tour of a plant in Japan to see how the Japanese manufacturing concepts of continuous improvement, or *kaizen*, are implemented.

Tour organizers said no one was allowed to take pictures, but someone in the group found one manufacturing method so interesting that he tried to take a picture of it secretly. One of the Japanese company managers saw it happen.

"Don't be afraid," he said. "Take as many pictures as you want. By the time you copy this and implement it, we will already have our next improved method."

This was eye-opening for a young, 30-year-old manager like me at the time. I realized it's all about competing with *yourself* and finding a way to better *yourself* always. This concept works in new product design, it works in operations, and it works with your own self-development.

Let's look at another example of how this mindset could have saved a company from disruption.

Kodak engineer Steve Sasson invented the first digital camera in 1975. But when he presented the new invention to management, management shut him down.

Kodak management thought of digital photography as the enemy. Kodak ignored digital cameras because, at the time, the company made its profits on film and paper. Customers would no longer need those items if Kodak switched to producing digital cameras.

It was a bad decision. Kodak went through a decades-long decline as digital photography destroyed its film-based business model.

Despite the fact a Kodak engineer invented the first digital camera, the leader's unwillingness to change in order to protect the old ways led to the company's failure.

If you have a better way to do things, why hide it? Someone else will invent it and destroy you anyway.

The company itself was not at fault—it was the leader's unwillingness to change that created those failures.

In 1989, Colby Chandler, then-CEO at Kodak, retired. The board had to choose between two top candidates for the next CEO. The choice came down to Phil Samper and Kay R. Whitmore. Whitmore was a fan of traditional film business, whereas Samper had a deep appreciation for digital technology. The board chose Whitmore.

Whitmore said he would "make sure Kodak stayed closer to its core businesses in film and photographic chemicals."[84]

Instead of spending so much time and effort on organizational transformations, leaders should be focusing on reinventing and changing themselves. Organizations will follow their lead.

Many lessons in history illustrate such downfalls.

Motorola once dominated the mobile phone industry with its analog phones. Eventually, it was replaced by Nokia, with its smaller digital mobile phones. But even that advantage didn't make Nokia win in the long run, as Samsung and Apple disrupted Nokia with smart phones.[85]

Change doesn't happen only once. It's constant. Leaders who stay ahead of the game learn to change their own behavior as well.

Successful leaders continue to reflect on themselves and practice self-leadership. They know once they manage themselves, their organization will change and emerge positively.

## HOW LEADERS CHANGE ORGANIZATIONS

A leader alone can't possibly see all the threats and uncertainties lurking around every corner. The entire organization must stay alert for risks and look for opportunities to reinvent themselves and become better every day.

But the organizational change starts with the leader.

## TACKLING COMPLEXITY

In today's complex business environment, organizations that do not adapt and evolve will fail to deliver on their commitments and, consequently, success. Change is necessary to stay relevant. As leaders make changes to their own habits, organizations become ready to embrace change and stay relevant.

Today, many organizations have mastered the structural side of change. It may make a lot of sense to call it *change management* because the focus on systems, structures, and processes is fairly mechanical.

But the real change happens on the people side of the business. How change is embraced depends on the people's values, behaviors, mindsets, and emotional connections with the leader. The real adaptation happens at this level deep down.

Who can connect to the people and keep them committed in organizational transformation despite the fears, uncertainties, and doubts? Only the leader can do this.

We spoke about what the leader should do. Maybe we should also talk about what a leader should not do in organizational transformation projects.

Big transformational projects usually come about because of a leader's personal opinions and interests. It may look like there is buy-in from all stakeholders, but more often people know where it really comes from. Outside approval isn't necessarily a bad thing—good leaders should have good ideas and give good direction.

But imagine if a bad leader comes up with a project simply to show off and impress their boss. Imagine a bad leader creates more work for everyone else but doesn't have any real value.

Generating ideas for the leader's own sake may help the leader get a promotion, but it distances the team from the leader. People can see through it.

It is key for good leaders not to attach any personal interest to organizational transformation efforts. Instead, leaders should get to know their own organization's strengths and weaknesses to make good decisions about transformations.

Let's take a look at an example.

At one point, a leader was trying to bring in an expensive, new program-management process with tools to make a major transformation to the way we did project management. He wanted to roll it out globally. The push all started when he saw one project fail due to the team not following the established process.

I had to take a stand against this move. We already had a great tool—the problem was this particular team didn't use it.

The leader did not have the knowledge and tried to overhaul an entire program-management process, which would have been a waste of time and money. Beyond that, he would have lost trust with his people who felt as if he doubted their capabilities.

Knowing the organizational capabilities and capacities helps leaders to know what is really required to get things done. Maybe that means introducing a whole new management process, but maybe it just means making sure every team is doing things the right way.

Again, it comes down to the organizational knowledge of the leader and being willing to change himself.

## THE LEADER EMBRACES THE SIILA MODEL

We started the discussion on the SIILA model with systems thinking, internalize, interact, learn, and concluded with adapt.

It's about the leader. The leader must be willing to engage in tough-love interactions with themselves for systems thinking and internalize it. They must be willing to engage with the tough-love interactions inside and outside the organization to learn. From the interactions they have, leaders learn what they don't know. Finally, leaders show tough love on themselves when they adapt.

## TACKLING COMPLEXITY

It's hard to change, but good leaders are committed to making it happen. When leaders go through this endless SIILA loop, they get the small things right. Each step can stop small issues from turning into big issues. The company develops a culture that embraces complexity and gets things done when the outcome is uncertain in the knowledge era.

# PART VI REVIEW

In part VI, we discussed the adapt part of the SIILA model in tackling complexity. Here are the key takeaways:

- In tackling complexity, the steps of systems thinking, internalize, and learn will not deliver results or help the leader get things done until the leader adapts with the knowledge gained.
- Leaders can adapt themselves by following four steps: (i) identify the knowledge gap, (ii) acquire the necessary knowledge, (iii) identify the individual change profile to develop a personal change plan, and (iv) make an unwavering commitment to change and adapt.
- The changing world in which leaders operate businesses today requires them to make a habit of reinventing themselves to create a better version of themselves. The organization will follow them, and as a result, leaders will continue to get things done and deliver on commitments time and time again.

In the final part of the book, we will put the SIILA model together in the endless cycle of lifelong learning and adapting.

# PART VII
# SIILA JOURNEY

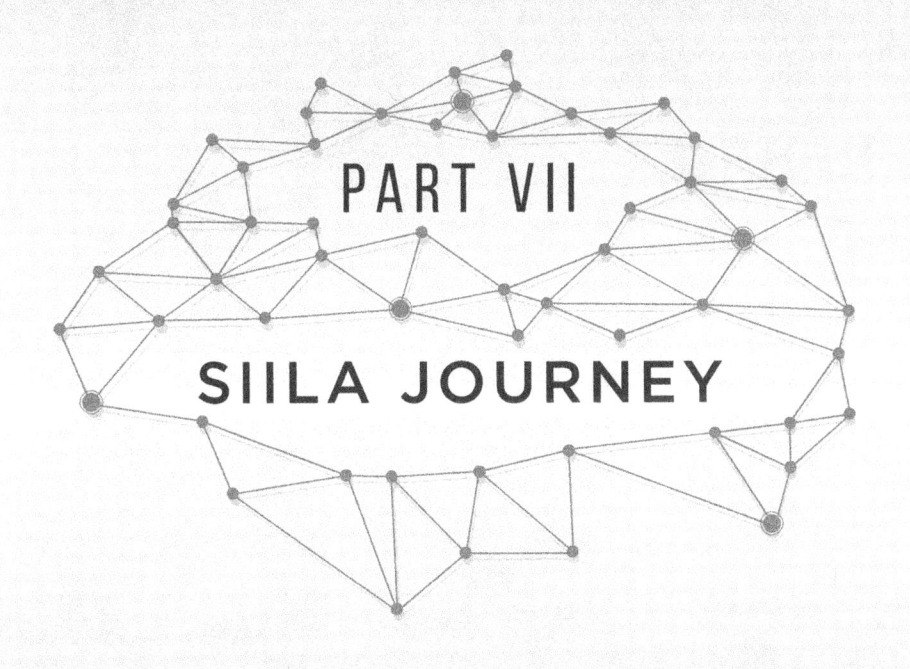

# CHAPTER 14

# THE SIILA LOOP NEVER ENDS—TURN KNOWLEDGE INTO SKILLS INTO HABITS

We began our journey together by accepting that organizations are complex adaptive systems, much like living organisms. People within each organization will continue to interact, be interdependent, learn, and evolve.

Leaders will gain leadership skills to get things done, whatever those objectives may be, but they can never stop learning. It is an ongoing, never-ending endeavor. If people and organizations continue to change, leaders must as well. Simply put, yesterday's skills cannot solve today's problems.

So, how are leaders supposed to keep up with all these changes?

The SIILA model presents a path forward. It is the solution to tackling complexity and getting things done. Within systems thinking, a leader must internalize, interact, learn, and adapt.

But leaders must remember that by the time they do adapt, things will have changed again. The ground is constantly shifting beneath our feet. So, leaders must begin the SIILA journey all over again.

This might sound painful, but it's not. If leaders internalize why the cycle is important, this new skill can become a habit. Soon enough, leaders won't even have to think about it.

## LEADERSHIP IS FORMING NEW HABITS

*We are what we repeatedly do.*
*Excellence, then, is not an act, but a habit.*
— Will Durant, paraphrasing Aristotle.[86]

Who we are is really the sum of our repeated habits. So, to be excellent means to develop excellent habits.

Habits go beyond knowledge, though knowledge is important. People gain knowledge in the classroom, by reading books, using the internet, and seeking out expert opinions. But that knowledge doesn't do anyone much good unless we apply it and use it until it becomes a skill.

To perform anything well, you need more than knowledge. Even a dean's list star student will need to develop and improve their skills, which can be a tedious task that requires much practice.

Think back to when you were learning to ride your bicycle for the first time. Your parents probably explained it to you. You probably watched your siblings, friends, or even someone on television ride. You saw how to do it, and it seemed pretty straightforward.

But as you worked to convert that knowledge into a skill you could use, you probably fell off the bike a few times. Suddenly you realized how hard it could be to stay balanced on two wheels! In those early moments, it felt as if there were a million different things to think about, from the placement of your hands, to your legs, to your balance. Those aspects didn't even account for steering in the right direction.

## THE SIILA LOOP NEVER ENDS—TURN KNOWLEDGE INTO SKILLS INTO HABITS

After a couple of scraped knees and bruises to your body and your ego, you eventually gained the skills necessary to ride a bike. Soon, you rode your bike to school alone for the first time. In that moment, you were proud of your accomplishment. You had come so far!

Excellence is not just a one-time thing. Excellence is what you do again and again. After a while, riding your bike becomes a habit. You ride to and from school without thinking about it. That act has become a habit. Now you can go learn a new good habit.

That is excellence.

There is an important lesson we can apply to leadership here. Let's go a little deeper to better understand the human brain and how it interprets knowledge, skills, and habits.

According to a study done by Dr. Bruce Lipton, a former professor of medicine at Stanford University, the conscious mind can process roughly 40 bits of information per second, while the subconscious mind can process more than 40 million bits of information per second.[87]

That means the subconscious mind is one million times faster than the conscious mind.

What does that distinction have to do with bicycles?

When you start learning something new—like riding a bicycle—you are completely focused on that task, using only the conscious mind. Remember, the conscious mind is slow, and it struggles to process everything.

When you fall down and scrape your knees, that's your conscious mind making mistakes and charting the course to develop this new skill. Your subconscious mind doesn't yet have a clue what's going on, so it stays quiet in the background.

With a lot of struggles, you are eventually able to repeat the skill often enough without failure that the conscious mind hands over that skill to the subconscious mind.

When that happens, you rock at riding a bike. It becomes second nature to you. That's when you start riding it like a pro. Maybe you talk on your cell phone while you ride or eat your breakfast with one hand while you steer with the other. Maybe you even stand on the seat to show off a little. You don't have to think about riding the bike anymore. It is unconscious competence.

Since the unconscious mind processes everything a million times faster than the conscious mind, does that sound like a habit to you?

A habit is simply an automatic response to a situation. You do it without even thinking about it, almost as if you have no control over it. It's an action you take so often that it becomes part of you.

The ability to master new skills and transform them into habits is the true excellence in leadership. It's not about one-time success. It's a continuous process of taking the right action without even thinking about it.

In complexity, everything around us is changing, including the leader himself. That's why the outcome is uncertain in the first place. The solution to tackling complexity is the leader's ability to continue to develop good habits to achieve true excellence.

What are the good leadership habits to develop?

There is no shortage of good leadership habits that one should develop. These may include integrity; transparency; honesty; initiative; vision; reliability; organization; discipline; respect; knowledge; attention to detail; cleanliness; a good smile; good listening, communication, decision-making, and thinking skills; an ability to develop people, take action, dress well, work out, interact with people, continue to learn; and more.

Most leaders know what is required in a general sense to be leader. Developing good habits is the tricky part.

## ON BECOMING UNCONSCIOUSLY COMPETENT

Becoming unconsciously competent is about transforming that knowledge into a skill and then into a habit. The easiest way to understand this transformation is with the four steps of competence building.

First, you don't know what you don't know. That's unconscious incompetence and is a dangerous place to be. If you behave as if you do know, nothing good will happen. You must quickly leave this phase.

Second, you know what you don't know. That is conscious incompetence. At this stage, you learn about what you don't know.

Third, you apply the knowledge you learned, you practice it, and you become good at it. That is conscious competence. You gained the skill, but you still have to think about it when you practice it. You have to be careful and deliberate. You start to grow as you continue to see repeated success.

Fourth is unconscious competence. At this stage, you can act without even thinking. You've consciously developed this skill, and now it is a habit processed in your unconscious mind.

Not all habits are good, though. You can develop bad habits with this process as well. Getting rid of them and replacing them with good habits can be difficult, but it's not impossible.

For example, maybe you grab a candy bar for a snack every day after lunch. It's habit. But one day you decide you want to lose some weight, and you must start to consciously change your habits. Before, you unconsciously threw a candy bar into your lunch box so that you would have it ready to go when the craving hit. You decide to ditch the candy bar habit and make healthier choices. Instead of putting a candy bar in your lunch box, you put an apple in there instead. At first, you have to think about it and make the choice. In the beginning, it's tough because you really want that candy bar. But over time, you throw the apple into your lunch box and don't even think about the candy bar anymore.

Many of the things we've talked about here seem small. One might wonder why it matters for leaders. Aren't they the ones doing big things and delegating small things to others in the organization?

The small things matter. Success comes when we get the small things right again, and again, and again.

Of course, leaders dream big, have big ideas, and have big plans. They must. But to accomplish those big things, leaders must focus on what they do today. If leaders are what they repeatedly do, they must develop good, productive habits.

Imagine a leader who has a habit of celebrating successes big and small but remains humble and curious—aware that they don't know what challenges they will face the next day. Imagine that same leader confronts failure without losing themselves completely. They learn from their mistakes. They get back on their feet. They don't make the same mistake again, and they are able to move on.

These are the characteristics of a healthy, resilient leader. The practice may sound very simple, but it's more difficult and less common than you'd think.

It requires leaders not only to understand that success rarely, if ever, happens in a straight line but also to accept that fact. Success involves many triumphs and failures, and good leaders can't afford to get caught up in the highs and lows of either.

If leaders can build this attitude into the organization, the entire organization will be set up to continually learn, evolve, and improve. If the entire organization stays alert to all the things that could go wrong, problems can be solved when they are small and manageable, which prevents those problems from growing to affect delivery of performance expectations.

## SIILA IS A HABIT

The challenge for today's leaders is this: How to get things done and deliver on expectations while not harming other aspects, such as the environment, society, people, culture, and long-term success. Leaders must get comfortable thinking about the whole, rather than their preferred parts, of leadership.

I have lived, studied, and worked around the world in Asia, Europe, and the United States. I've managed large global businesses. I have experienced

## THE SIILA LOOP NEVER ENDS—TURN KNOWLEDGE INTO SKILLS INTO HABITS

great leadership in both the Western and Eastern worlds. I've also studied leadership on three continents.

With this breadth of experience, I came to realize the answer to leadership in a complexity paradigm is to combine the best of Eastern and Western leadership principles. Getting results and getting things done remain the core themes. And to get them, today's leaders must continually use the SIILA model. They must start by adopting the key philosophies of systems thinking and internalizing. Then they can continually interact, learn, and adapt.

Since people and organizations are complex, there is no alternative to achieve continued success. Leaders must make a habit of cycling through the SIILA model.

During the whole cycle, the leader is part of the organization and not on top of the organization. That view is a fundamental shift from old leader-follower methods of leadership.

To wrap up, here are the five steps of the never-ending SIILA loop with its key elements:

1. **Systems thinking**
   - Understanding the interconnectivity of the organization
   - Accountability for everything that happens in the organization
   - Emerging positively or negatively based on the behavior of the leader
2. **Internalize**
   - Understanding the power of mind
   - Motivations for leadership
   - The power of mastering yourself
3. **Interact**
   - Tough-love interactions
   - Knowing your people and the organization
   - Escalation case studies

4. **Learn**
    - Always learning
    - The power of teaching
    - Teachable point of view
5. **Adapt**
    - Individual change profile
    - Reinventing yourself
    - Changing organizations

The SIILA model leverages the best of Eastern and Western leadership philosophies to provide a path forward for leaders to tackle complexity with tough-love interactions when the outcome is uncertain in the knowledge era.

With this knowledge, today's leaders can begin to practice what will become a skill. As they repeat it in a never-ending loop, it will become a habit. SIILA is a habit that will never go bad; it will continue to be useful and relevant as we tackle complexity to get things done.

If SIILA becomes a habit for a leader, the leader himself will transform into a complexity leader. He will be less stressed because his motivations and value system are aligned with what he does. The subconscious mind will soon take over and do the heavy lifting, freeing up a leader's conscious mind for other things.

The effect will allow leaders to transform the entire organization, creating a culture and value system where the leader is the role model. These skills the leader gains to tackle complexity are transferable then.

No matter what failures or unexpected difficulties pop up, complexity leaders move on with these habits:

- systems thinking,
- internalize,
- interact,
- learn, and
- adapt.

## THE SIILA LOOP NEVER ENDS—TURN KNOWLEDGE INTO SKILLS INTO HABITS

As a result, leaders will never lose to themselves. They will continue to thrive in life and at work because their value systems and their habits are aligned.

Their continual learning and adaptation become their greatest assets because they will make them successful in subsequent endeavors.

Complexity leaders naturally become mindful and more productive as they live in the present and take appropriate action now with focus and clarity.

## CHAPTER 15

## MY SIILA JOURNEY

In late 2012, I was one of the final two candidates for a senior executive role in a global industrial company. At the time, I was 42 years old, working as the vice president of a global business unit based in Hong Kong.

In the final step in the hiring process, I flew out to visit the company headquarters in Minneapolis in the United States. To my surprise, the company arranged two full days of interviews with psychologists to complete the psychological evaluation for the job.

I had taken personality assessment tests and other forms of psychological evaluations for job interviews in the past, but they involved online tests, essays, short discussions, and role-playing. Those online tests would typically produce a report on personality style, thinking style, interpersonal relationships, and conflict resolution. But the assessments at this company's headquarters were much more intense.

Three senior psychologists, all appearing to be in their late 60s, met with me. They created a really comfortable, cozy environment that felt like home. Then, they started asking me questions. Where did I grow up?

What was my family like? What primary school did I attend? What did I remember most from first grade?

It didn't feel like an interview. Instead, it felt as if I was having a conversation with older relatives in my family. I felt at ease and comfortable with them, even though I had never done that kind of self-reflection before.

They asked me how I would describe my grandfather and grandmother and what kind of influence they had on me.

I recalled how my grandparents planted trees in our garden in their old age even though they knew they would never live to enjoy the fruit from those trees. They valued simplicity, discipline, and connectivity to their community and to nature. Those things were baked into their daily lives.

They asked about my parents and their childhoods.

During World War II, after Singapore fell to the Japanese in 1942, Sri Lanka became the central base for British operations in Southeast Asia. India demanded the British guarantee independence for their support during the war, while Sri Lanka committed wholeheartedly to the Allied war effort.

Because Sri Lanka was an indispensable strategic location in the Indian Ocean, it was a popular military target for the Japanese, increasing tensions after the British established their central base in the area. The whole island was under military jurisdiction during the war.[88]

During that time, my parents were growing up in the central farmlands of Sri Lanka. My father had completed middle school. My grandparents chose not to send my mother to school for her safety.

One psychologist asked me what I learned from my father and how that affects the way I lead today.

## THAT COCONUT TREE AND LESSONS FROM MY PARENTS

We lived in a large farmhouse in the middle of a coconut plantation, right next to a big rice paddy field. My mother was a great cook, but my father had demanding tastes. He loved coconut. No meal lacked the fruit.

One day, my mother ran out of coconut. We usually had several workers come out to pluck coconuts from our own field, but that day my father couldn't find any workers.

In his mind, this was an emergency.

He made a foot strap with a rag and started climbing a tall coconut tree to pluck some coconuts himself. At eight years old, I could not believe my eyes.

After he descended from the tree, with plenty of coconuts for our next several meals, I said, "I didn't know you could climb coconut trees. I have never seen you do it before. How did you do that?"

"Son," he said, "you never ask anyone to do anything you cannot do yourself."

This lesson has been the foundation of my entire journey—from school, to leadership, to life itself.

It's not about having to do it all by yourself; rather, it's about your ability to roll up your sleeves and do the work when you need to. It's about knowing the details and what it takes to get the job done.

And learning what it takes to get the job done takes time. I was fortunate enough not to parachute into the corner office too early. Instead, I worked up from ground zero. I began as an engineer, and I always felt comfortable working with details and people. During a crisis, I could roll up my sleeves and help my team with hands-on support, whether it meant helping during an operational crisis on the production shop floor, facing a tough customer, or helping out with personal matters.

Over the years, my style has built an enormous amount of trust and credibility within every organization I led. They knew I knew the details. They knew I was willing to get my hands dirty, teach, and support when necessary. I was always part of the team and could fill in any seat to help or cover for my team.

## MODEL WHAT YOU KNOW

When my father climbed the coconut tree, I realized there is no power in the positions you hold. The power comes from the knowledge you gain and the skills you develop. Knowledge is power.

My mother worked hard to support my father with his business while also taking care of nine children. It was a daunting task, but she was an iron lady up to the challenge. What I remember most about her, though, was her ability to connect with anyone. She helped people and treated everyone equally.

During my childhood, I remember many older, underprivileged folks would come to stay in our house. We never ran out of visitors. My mother took care of them and helped them in any way she could, even if she didn't have enough for herself. There were days, I remember, when she gave her own food to someone she thought needed it more. Her kindness, combined with her ability to connect with people, was an amazing gift.

Even though she did not attend school, her knowledge about life, her courage, and her ability to deeply understand people's feelings were inspiring.

At the age of 75, she went on to lead a tea plantation with her nephew. They built a beautiful mountain house by hand, employed only local labor, and refused to use machinery to get it done. She wanted to contribute to the community, not just start a business.

Though my parents were great inspirations to me, they both suffered greatly throughout their lives. Their childhoods were full of fear and sorrow. The country's civil war, which began in 1983 and ended in 2009 with 100,000 people dead, cast a shadow over their adult lives too.

These hardships made my parents stronger and helped them discover who they were. They continued to learn to adapt and survive during difficult times while raising nine children.

I've experienced my own share of painful hardships and failures in my own life. Knowing that my parents experienced what they did and were still able to be great role models inspires me to do the work I do today.

## MY FAILURES AND CYCLES OF LEARNING

Despite the extensive psychological exam, I did not get that senior executive role I interviewed for in Minneapolis.

The job was for a president in the Asia Pacific region. At my last dinner with the chairman of the board during the interview process, I asked why the job was based in Hong Kong.

"Shouldn't it be in Shanghai to be closer to the customers and the operations?" I asked.

He told me then it was for historical reasons—but my question made him think. They offered the job to the other finalist, who was already based in Shanghai.

That seemed like a failure at first, but it worked out perfectly for me. Three months later, Johnson Electric moved me to Switzerland to lead the automotive division with multiple global business units under me. Because I didn't get the job in Shanghai, I was able to live, work, and study in Europe. I gained a tremendous amount of exposure and experience. So, the whole sequence of events was a win-win.

## CAPITALIZE ON YOUR PAST

My father had a very close association with the Buddhist temple, so while I grew up, my family went to the temple regularly. Once there was a procession from the temple going through the villages, and people were donating all sorts of things in reverence to the temple. As a Buddhist, one of the highest gifts one can donate, or *wessantara puja*, is his own children.

My father decided to donate me to the temple.

Traditionally, this meant I had to be ordained to become a monk and had to stay at the temple. I was 12 years old.

So, I went to the temple. That night at the temple, I remember all kinds of chanting and other activities.

It was big news in the village that my father donated a son and that I would become a monk.

The next day, my schoolteachers and other expert monks came to talk to my father. I was excited to be a monk, but I was also one of the top performers in school at that time, and my teachers thought I had a future in academics.

The monks spoke with my father and told him that after a *puja*, I didn't actually have to become a monk. That was the traditional path, but they argued that I could contribute more to society if I studied well and helped to make the world a better place while still embodying the societal and cultural values.

So, they brought me back to school and let me pick my formal education.

I'm really proud of my parents' decision to dedicate me to the family faith. I'm also proud of their decision to take a totally different path. They took a nontraditional path, and it took guts to do that.

After this upheaval, I somehow failed to get enough marks to pass the primary school scholarship exam. As a result, I could not go onto a national school to study my middle school curriculum.

On the surface, that outcome might look like a failure. After all, I did leave the temple to study hard and become a good student. But it actually worked out perfectly. I went to a middle school about three miles away from my family home. I could ride my bicycle to it every day. I also enjoyed another five great years living in the unspoiled nature of the village before needing to leave for the city for future education. I cherish that time.

At that school, I passed the middle school national exam with the best results the school ever recorded. My parents were able to send me to one of the top high schools in the country. I did really well there, went to university, and got a degree in electrical and electronic engineering with honors.

It was in middle school that I discovered I loved to teach. I often helped teach at the primary school, and sometimes the principal would even send me to teach classes if the teacher couldn't come in that day. I often tutored kids in the evenings.

In university, many students had a hard time following the professors' English lectures. I would repeat the same lecture in simpler ways, with more examples, in local languages to help my fellow classmates. These tutoring sessions were so popular that some students stopped attending their normal classes and just came for my tutoring sessions at night.

I never charged for my tutoring sessions, and I never worried I was teaching my competition to be better than I was in class. I felt it was valuable to share knowledge and help others. I realized my knowledge improved, too, every time I taught. Many of my classmates would say I was destined to be a professor someday.

After graduation, I connected with Professor Paul Hoole, a brilliant teacher who had his doctorate degree from Oxford University. He taught artificial intelligence, neural networks, and more to us. Later, he left Sri Lanka and joined Nanyang Technological University in Singapore.

He invited me to come to Singapore to present one of our research papers at a conference in Singapore. After I arrived, he asked me why I didn't find a job in industry in Singapore. It was 1997 then. So, I started working in the industry in Singapore and began a whole different journey in my industrial career.

Beyond the time Professor Hoole devoted to engineering, teaching, and research, he also spent time studying and teaching the Bible in seminaries and churches. On several occasions, he practiced as a pastor. Professor Hoole's excellent teaching style and strong faith is forever etched in my mind.

In Singapore, I became a research and development engineer at Eutech Instruments, which later became part of Thermo Fisher Scientific, designing electronic circuits and writing embedded systems software for scientific instruments. But soon I found out that electrical engineering is not enough to perform product design, and I needed the knowledge of mechanical engineering. I attended night school at the National University of Singapore and received a master's degree in mechatronics.

Two years later, I was interviewed for a senior design engineer job at Data Storage Institute (DSI), a Singapore government agency that conducts research on computer hard disks. I received the job offer via letter, which proposed a start date but was conditional on successfully passing a medical examination.

I had never had any medical issues, and I was young, so I was confident I'd get the job. I resigned from the job I had and went for the medical examination. I was shocked when the results came back. I was color-blind. I didn't know that before I took the test. I knew I wasn't good at painting and was never a fan of art—that's why I did engineering instead—but I didn't know I was color-blind.

A few weeks later, DSI sent a letter home saying that I failed the medical exam and the color-code test. As a result, the job offer was no longer valid. I was suddenly jobless, living in a two-bedroom apartment with my wife and nine-month-old daughter, Lawanya. At the time, we were living paycheck to paycheck, like most young couples.

At first glance, the situation seemed like a terrible move on my part. And it sure felt like that at the time. But it ended up being one of the best things to ever happen to me. The whole computer hard disk industry declined, and DSI was dissolved several years later.[89]

I got a new job in Delphi, Singapore, as a systems engineer designing electronic controls for cars. I worked my way up to lead multiple global programs as well as the definition of future product portfolios.

Delphi promoted and moved me to Kokomo, Indiana, USA, where I worked in several places including Milwaukee, Wisconsin, and in Auburn Hills, Michigan. I was on track to be a general manager. But I realized I had to get an MBA to fill in my knowledge gap, particularly on finance, economics, and business law. I completed my MBA from Kelly School of Business at Indiana University and my masters in global management from Thunderbird School of Global Management. I was always looking for ways to learn. I learned from everyone I came across and also completed formal education as necessary.

I managed the turnaround of several businesses, started new product lines, held positions as a global president, managing director, and general manager. I communicated well across cultures. After all, I *am* color-blind. I realized it was the best gift I ever had in leading global businesses. I learned how to connect with people as humans, regardless of color, age, and gender.

I later moved to Hong Kong with Johnson Electric. There, I had the pleasure to work for Patrick Wang, CEO and chairman, who truly embodied what it means to be an owner of the business. It was an excellent experience. I was inspired and motivated by his passion and energy. I did well as the vice president of the global engine and transmission management business, and he promoted me and sent me to Switzerland to manage the entire automotive division with multiple global business units.

I became curious as to why some leaders were successful while others failed miserably. That's when I started to research the differences, which eventually turned into my doctorate in complexity leadership.

I stayed very humble, looking for every opportunity to learn. I knew that learning was critical for success—and that to learn, I would have to face many difficult situations in which I didn't know the answer. And I did.

After a successful six years at Johnson Electric in Switzerland, I returned home to Asia and to Delphi, which later became Aptiv.

There have been plenty of failures in my life. The lessons from all those failures, from the classroom to the boardroom, made me stronger.

## LIFELONG LEARNING IN LEADERSHIP

Ram Charan was first introduced to the world of business while working for his family's shoe shop in a small town in northern India, where he was raised. As a boy, Ram delivered shoes to clients all around the city.

He later went on to get an engineering degree in India, as well as an MBA and doctorate degrees from Harvard Business School. He served on the faculties of Harvard Business School and Northwestern University.

Ram Charan became a world-renowned business adviser, author, and speaker, spending 40 years working with many of the top companies, CEOs, and boards of our time.[90]

## TACKLING COMPLEXITY

Ram still uses his lessons from the shoe shop where he worked as a boy. He often speaks about how well the shoe shop knew its customers. It knew exactly what they wanted, how their shoes should fit, and how each client needed to be treated.[91]

Many great leaders, from Ram Dass to Steve Jobs to Ram Charan, discussed in this book share their stories, their leadership point of view, and their teachable point of view.

Are they born to lead, teach, or advise on leadership? Or did they learn how to do it?

The debate over whether leaders are born or raised will never end. But we cannot afford to do nothing, just waiting to discover if we're lucky enough to be successful leaders or lucky enough to get hired by a successful leader.

From my own experience growing up in a small village in central Sri Lanka, I've found that only hard work and continual learning helped me figure out how to lead. I truly believe that the harder I work, the luckier I get.

Who we are is a result of our values and beliefs, which are shaped from the sum of our experiences. If we keep our learning mode switched on, we can continue to learn, grow, and reinvent ourselves for the better. We can become successful leaders at work and in our personal life.

The world we live in will continue to be characterized by volatility, uncertainty, complexity, and ambiguity.

> *There is no way to bring certainty and determinism back to our life and work. We can only learn and adapt continuously to lead through these uncertainties.*
>
> *I conclude that the ability for a leader to tackle complexity comes down to having the <u>right mindset</u> and <u>getting the small things done</u> that matter most, right – in life and at work.*

It's not what you know today that's going to help you tackle complexities tomorrow. It's how much you are willing to interact, learn, and adapt. Having lived, studied, and worked around the world for over 25 years, bridging the best of Eastern and Western approaches to leadership, the best of hands-on experience and academic knowledge, I am presenting SIILA as a concept to change the way we think in order to cultivate our learning. I hope to change our mindset to fit the modern era and all its demands. Will you join me?

# ENDNOTES

1. Sam Shead, "The Global Chip Shortage Is Starting to Have Major Real-World Consequences," CNBC, May 7, 2021, https://www.cnbc.com/2021/05/07/chip-shortage-is-starting-to-have-major-real-world-consequences.html.
2. "Airbus Scraps A380 Superjumbo Jet as Sales Slump," BBC, February 18, 2019, https://www.bbc.com/news/business-47231504.
3. Matthew S. Schwartz, "Airbus to Stop Production of A380 Superjumbo Jet," NPR, accessed February 14, 2019, https://www.npr.org/2019/02/14/694620105/airbus-to-stop-production-of-a380-superjumbo-jet.
4. Frederick Taylor, *The Principles of Scientific Management* (New York: Harper & Brothers, 1911).
5. "Frederick Winslow Taylor," The British Library, accessed November 18, 2021, https://www.bl.uk/people/frederick-winslow-taylor.
6. "Great Man Theory," The Decision Lab, accessed November 8, 2021, https://thedecisionlab.com/reference-guide/anthropology/great-man-theory/.
7. Kendra Cherry, "Understanding the Trait Theory of Leadership," Very Well Mind, March 8, 2021, https://www.verywellmind.com/what-is-the-trait-theory-of-leadership-2795322.

8  Indeed Editorial Team, "What Is Behavioral Leadership Theory? Definition and Types of Behavioral Leadership," Indeed, February 22, 2021, https://www.indeed.com/career-advice/career-development/behavioral-leadership-theory.

9  "What Is Transactional Leadership? How Structure Leads to Results," St. Thomas University, May 8, 2018, https://online.stu.edu/articles/education/what-is-transactional-leadership.aspx.

10  Indeed Editorial Team, "Understanding the Contingency Theory of Leadership," Indeed, December 3, 2020, https://www.indeed.com/career-advice/career-development/contingency-theory-of-leadership.

11  Kendra Cherry, "What Is Transformational Leadership Theory?" Very Well Mind, March 4, 2020, https://www.verywellmind.com/what-is-transformational-leadership-2795313.

12  Rian M. Gorey, David R. Dobat, and Linda Booth Sweeney, "Managing in the Knowledge Era," Systems Thinker, accessed November 9, 2021, https://thesystemsthinker.com/managing-in-the-knowledge-era/.

13  Peter F. Drucker, "Knowledge-Worker Productivity: The Biggest Challenge," California Management Review 41, no. 1 (Winter 1999): 79–94, https://cmr.berkeley.edu/search/articleDetail.aspx?article=4872.

14  "Derek Chauvin Sentenced for Murder of George Floyd," CNN, accessed November 18, 2021, https://www.cnn.com/videos/us/2021/06/25/derek-chauvin-sentencing-sot-vpx.cnn.

15  Rakesh Kochhar, "Unemployment Rose Higher in Three Months of COVID-19 Than It Did in Two Years of the Great Recession," Pew Research Center, June 11, 2020, https://www.pewresearch.org/fact-tank/2020/06/11/unemployment-rose-higher-in-three-months-of-covid-19-than-it-did-in-two-years-of-the-great-recession/.

16  Claudio Fernando-Araoz, "Jack Welch's Approach to Leadership," *Harvard Business Review*, March 3, 2020, https://hbr.org/2020/03/jack-welchs-approach-to-leadership.

# ENDNOTES

17 Catherine Clifford, "Jack Welch: This Is the No. 1 Key to Success as a Leader," CNBC, November 17, 2017, https://www.cnbc.com/2017/11/17/former-ge-ceo-jack-welch-how-to-be-a-great-leader.html.

18 "Textiles-Related Business," Toyota, accessed November 18, 2021, https://www.toyota-global.com/company/history_of_toyota/75years/text/taking_on_the_automotive_business/chapter2/section6/item1_b.html.

19 Matt Leonard, "Toyota, Citing Lessons Learned from 2011 Earthquake, Expects No Major Semiconductor Impact," Supply Chain Dive, May 14, 2021, https://www.supplychaindive.com/news/toyota-semiconductor-shortage-earthquake-inventory-ihs-gartner-forecast-2022/600193/.

20 Hirotaka Takeuchi, Emi Osono, and Norihiko Shimizu, "The Contradictions That Drive Toyota's Success," *Harvard Business Review*, June 2008, https://hbr.org/2008/06/the-contradictions-that-drive-toyotas-success.

21 "Executive Biography of Dennis A. Muilenburg," Aerospace Pioneers, Boeing, accessed November 18, 2021, https://www.boeing.com/history/pioneers/dennis-a-muilenburg.page.

22 "Analyst Reaction to Boeing Investors Day," Leeham News and Analysis, May 12, 2016, https://leehamnews.com/2016/05/12/analyst-reaction-boeing-investors-day/.

23 Scott David, Carter Copeland, and Rob Wertheimer, *Lessons from the Titans* (New York: McGraw Hill, 2020), 72–75.

24 Dominic Gates, "Boeing Creates New In-house Avionics Unit, Reversing Years of Outsourcing," *Seattle Times*, July 31, 2017, https://www.seattletimes.com/business/boeing-aerospace/boeing-setting-up-new-in-house-unit-to-build-avionics-controls/.

25 "Summary of the FAA's Review of the Boeing 737 Max," Federal Aviation Administration, November 18, 2020, https://www.faa.gov/foia/electronic_reading_room/boeing_reading_room/media/737_RTS_Summary.pdf.

26 William Langewische, "What Really Brought Down the Boeing 737 Max?," *New York Times*, September 18, 2019, https://www.nytimes.com/2019/09/18/magazine/boeing-737-max-crashes.html.

27 "Airworthiness Certification," Federal Aviation Administration, accessed November 8, 2021, https://www.faa.gov/aircraft/air_cert/airworthiness_certification.

28 Leslie Josephs and Amelia Lucas, "Boeing Fires CEO Dennis Muilenburg, as the Company Struggles with 737 Max Crisis," CNBC, December 23, 2019, https://www.cnbc.com/2019/12/23/boeing-stock-halted-pending-news-company-battles-fallout-737-max-crisis.html.

29 "About: Cynefin Framework," DBPedia, accessed November 18, 2021, https://dbpedia.org/page/Cynefin_framework.

30 "Gaia Hypothesis," Science Direct, accessed November 8, 2021, https://www.sciencedirect.com/topics/earth-and-planetary-sciences/gaia-hypothesis.

31 The Investopedia team, "Environmental, Social and Governance (ESG) Criteria," Investopedia, March 5, 2021, https://www.investopedia.com/terms/e/environmental-social-and-governance-esg-criteria.asp.

32 "He Who Opens a School Door, Closes a Prison," Relief Web, November 19, 2013, https://reliefweb.int/report/iran-islamic-republic/he-who-opens-school-door-closes-prison.

33 Lance Lochner and Enrico Moretti, "The Effect of Education on Crime: Evidence from Prison Inmates, Arrests, and Self-Reports," University of California, Berkeley, March 2004, https://eml.berkeley.edu/~moretti/lm46.pdf.

34 Gabe Gutierrez, Rich Gardella, Kevin Monahan, and Talesha Reynolds, "GM Chose Not to Implement Fix for Ignition Problem," CNBC, March 14, 2014, https://www.cnbc.com/2014/03/14/gm-chose-not-to-implement-fix-for-ignition-problem.html.

35 Jonathan Stempel, "GM Reaches Settlement over Lost Vehicle Value from Defective Ignition Switches," Reuters, March 27, 2020, https://

# ENDNOTES

www.reuters.com/article/us-gm-settlement/gm-reaches-settlement-over-lost-vehicle-value-from-defective-ignition-switches-idUSK-BN21E3LG.

36 Jonathan Stempel, "GM Reaches Settlement over Lost Vehicle Value from Defective Ignition Switches," Reuters, February 27, 2020, https://www.reuters.com/article/us-gm-settlement/gm-reaches-settlement-over-lost-vehicle-value-from-defective-ignition-switches-idUSKBN21E3LG.

37 Emma Seppala and Kim Cameron, "Proof That Positive Work Cultures Are More Productive," *Harvard Business Review*, December 1, 2015, https://hbr.org/2015/12/proof-that-positive-work-cultures-are-more-productive.

38 "Ninety Percent of an Iceberg Is below the Waterline," USGS, accessed November 8, 2021, https://www.usgs.gov/media/images/ninety-percent-iceberg-below-waterline.

39 "Jeffrey Jensen Arnett," Jeffrey Jensen Arnett, accessed November 8, 2021, http://jeffreyarnett.com.

40 "Great Responsibilities and New Global Power," The National WWII Museum New Orleans, October 23, 2020, https://www.nationalww2museum.org/war/articles/new-global-power-after-world-war-ii-1945.

41 Evelyn Cheng and Yen Nee Lee, "New Chart Shows China Could Overtake the U.S. as the World's Largest Economy Earlier than Expected," CNBC, December 31, 2021, https://www.cnbc.com/2021/02/01/new-chart-shows-china-gdp-could-overtake-us-sooner-as-covid-took-its-toll.html.

42 "Kendrick B. Melrose: Caring About People: Employees and Customers," Ethix, October 1, 2007, https://ethix.org/2007/10/01/caring-about-people-employees-and-customers.

43 "Thunderbird Oath of Honor," Oath of Honor, Thunderbird School of Global Management, accessed November 8, 2021, https://thunderbird.asu.edu/about/global-impact/thunderbird-oath-honor.

44 Weragoda Sarada Maha Thero, *Treasury of Truth: Illustrated Dhammapada* (Singapore: The Singapore Buddhist Meditation Centre: 1993).

45 Lao Tzu, *Tao Te Ching: The Classic Book of Integrity and the Way* (New York: Bantam, 1990).

46 Gabe Paoletti, "Meet Hiroo Onoda, the Soldier Who Kept Fighting World War II for 29 Years after It Ended," All That's Interesting, July 12, 2021, https://allthatsinteresting.com/hiroo-onoda.

47 Anna Katalin Aklan, "Inspired by Gandhi: Mahatma Gandhi's Influence on Significant Leaders of Nonviolence," History in Flux 2, no. 2 (2020): 115–124, https://doi.org/10.32728/flux.2020.2.6.

48 Mind Tools Content Team, "Understanding the Dark Triad," Mind Tools, accessed November 8, 2021, https://www.mindtools.com/pages/article/understanding-dark-triad.htm.

49 "Dark Triad," Science Direct, accessed November 8, 2021, https://www.sciencedirect.com/topics/psychology/dark-triad.

50 Val Willingham, "Shades of Gray: What Happens to Presidents' Hair," CNN, January 22, 2013, https://www.cnn.com/2013/01/22/health/presidents-gray/.

51 "Perspective," The Drucker Institute, accessed November 8, 2021, https://www.drucker.institute/perspective/about-peter-drucker/.

52 "Peter Drucker Biography," The Famous People, accessed November 9, 2021, https://www.thefamouspeople.com/profiles/peter-drucker-132.php.

53 "Dasa-rājādhamma/10 Royal Virtues," Suttas, accessed November 19, 2021, http://www.suttas.com/dasa-r257j257dhamma--10-royal-virtues.html.

54 "Confucius, the Analects – 13," USC US-China Institute, USC Annenberg, accessed November 9, 2021, https://china.usc.edu/confucius-analects-13.

55 Sun Tzu, *The Art of War* (Mankato, MN: Capstone Publishing, 2010).

# ENDNOTES

56 Shawn Langlois and Padraic Cassidy, "Ford's 2006 Loss Totals Record 12.7 Billion," Market Watch, January 25, 2007, https://www.marketwatch.com/story/ford-posts-huge-loss-but-new-ceo-gets-high-marks.

57 "How Alan Mulally Unleashed the Accelerating Power of Alignment," *The Shiftpoints Blog*, Shiftpoints, October 1, 2019, https://www.shiftpoints.com/blog/how-alan-mulally-unleashed-the-accelerating-power-of-alignment.

58 "Organizational Culture Change Example – Alan Mulally Ford Turnaround Story," New Age Leadership, accessed November 9, 2021, https://newageleadership.com/organizational-culture-change. https://www.kornferry.com/insights/briefings-magazine/issue-20/alan-mulally-man-who-saved-ford.

59 D.M. Collins, "Was Brutus Really Julius Caesar's Son?" History, A Rose in a Prose, April 24, 2018, https://arroseinaprose.org/2018/04/24/was-brutus-really-julius-caesars-son/.

60 Chip Cutter, "Warren Buffet Says Bad Leaders Pose Biggest Risk to Companies," *Wall Street Journal*, May 3, 2021, https://www.wsj.com/articles/warren-buffett-says-bad-leaders-pose-biggest-risk-to-companies-11620034201.

61 Jim Kershner, "Boeing and Washington's Aerospace Industry, 1934-2015," History Link, September 8, 2015, https://www.historylink.org/File/11111.

62 George L. Kelling and James Q. Wilson, "Broken Windows," *Atlantic*, March 1982, https://www.theatlantic.com/magazine/archive/1982/03/broken-windows/304465/.

63 "Analysis of the Sumatra-Andaman Earthquake Reveals Longest Fault Rupture Ever," National Science Foundation, accessed November 18, 2021, https://www.nsf.gov/news/news_summ.jsp?cntn_id=104179.

64 Jim Lucas, "Newton's Laws of Motion," September 26, 2017, https://www.livescience.com/46558-laws-of-motion.html.

65 Jan Hilgevoord and Jos Uffink, "The Uncertainty Principle," Stanford Encyclopedia of Philosophy, October 10, 2016, https://plato.stanford.edu/cgi-bin/encyclopedia/archinfo.cgi?entry=qt-uncertainty.

66 Christof Koch, "How Physics and Neuroscience Dictate Your 'Free' Will," *Scientific American*, May 1, 2012, https://www.scientificamerican.com/article/finding-free-will/.

67 Andrew Edgecliffe-Johnson "Larry Culp Looks for a Repeat Revolution at GE," August 15, 2021, https://www.ft.com/content/ff7e9ae0-c58d-11e8-bc21-54264d1c4647.

68 "Danaher Business System," How We Work, Danaher, accessed November 9, 2021, https://www.danaher.com/how-we-work/danaher-business-system.

69 Christopher Isidore, "These Are the Mistakes That Cost Boeing CEO Dennis Muilenburg His Job," CNN, December 24, 2019, https://edition.cnn.com/2019/12/24/business/boeing-dennis-muilenburg-mistakes/index.html.

70 Dan Roberts, "How (and Why) Great CIOs Lead through Teaching," The CIO Whisperers, August 4, 2020, https://www.cio.com/article/3569051/how-and-why-great-cios-lead-through-teaching.html.

71 Roshan Thiran, "Understanding Why Great Leaders Go to Great Length to Teach Others," Leaderonomics, May 20, 2016, https://www.leaderonomics.com/articles/leadership/why-great-leaders-teach-others.

72 "Boeing Names 3M Chief McNerney as CEO," NBC News, June 30, 2005, https://www.nbcnews.com/id/wbna8415508.

73 Dominic Gates, Kristi Heim, and Melissa Allison, "Mulally Jumps to Ford; 2 Boeing Veterans Step Up," *Seattle Times*, September 6, 2006, https://www.seattletimes.com/business/mulally-jumps-to-ford-2-boeing-veterans-step-up/.

74 Minda Zetlin, "Ram Dass, Who Inspired Steve Jobs to Visit India, Had a Very Simple Lesson for All of Us," Inc., accessed November 9, 2021, https://www.inc.com/minda-zetlin/ram-dass-influenced-steve-jobs-be-here-now.html.

# ENDNOTES

75 Ram Dass, "From the Archive: Ram Dass Speaks about Maharaji for the First Time," accessed November 9, 2021, https://www.ramdass.org/from-the-archive-ram-dass-speaks-about-maharaji-for-the-first-time/.

76 Minda Zetlin, "Ram Dass, Who Inspired Steve Jobs to Visit India, Had a Very Simple Lesson for All of Us," Inc., accessed November 9, 2021, https://www.inc.com/minda-zetlin/ram-dass-influenced-steve-jobs-be-here-now.html.

77 "Trip to India as Teen Was a Life-Changer for Steve Jobs," International, *India Times*, October 7, 2021, https://economictimes.indiatimes.com/news/international/trip-to-india-as-teen-was-a-life-chanfor-steve-jobs/articleshow/10264889.cms.

78 "Trip to India as Teen Was a Life-Changer for Steve Jobs," International, *India Times*, October 7, 2011, https://economictimes.indiatimes.com/news/international/trip-to-india-as-teen-was-a-life-changer-for-steve-jobs/articleshow/10264889.cms.

79 "Apple Co-founder Steve Jobs Dies," History, accessed November 19, 2021, https://www.history.com/this-day-in-history/apple-founder-steve-jobs-dies.

80 Ron Carucci, "Organizations Can't Change If Leaders Can't Change with Them," *Harvard Business Review*, October 24, 2016, https://hbr.org/2016/10/organizations-cant-change-if-leaders-cant-change-with-them.

81 Carol Harper, "Everyone Thinks of Changing the World, but No One Thinks of Changing Himself," Pain Pathways, July 16, 2015, https://www.painpathways.org/everyone-thinks-of-changing-the-world-but-no-one-thinks-of-changing-himself-leo-tolstoy/.

82 Daniella Whyte, "The 5 Reasons People Resist Change and What We Can Do about It," Inc., accessed November 9, 2021, https://www.inc.com/daniella-whyte/5-reasons-people-resist-change-and-what-we-can-do-about-it.html.

83 Ian Leslie, "The Subtle Reason Why Leaders Ignore Their Own Advice," BBC, April 21, 2020, https://www.bbc.com/worklife/article/20200420-the-subtle-reasons-why-leaders-ignore-their-own-advice.

84 Chunka Mui, "How Kodak Failed," *Forbes*, January 18, 2012, https://www.forbes.com/sites/chunkamui/2012/01/18/how-kodak-failed/?sh=74765a406f27.

85 "Why We Fail to See When We're About to Fail," *Forbes*, August 22, 2008, https://www.forbes.com/2008/08/22/summer-reading-motorola-ent-manage-cx_kw_0822whartoncellphone.html?sh=5073d00f329f.

86 Caelen Huntress, "My Favorite Quote of All Time Is a Misattribution," Mission Originals, August 24, 2017, https://medium.com/the-mission/my-favourite-quote-of-all-time-is-a-misattribution-66356f22843d.

87 Susan Garguilo, "The Key to Your Next Promotion? Paper and Crayons," CNN, April 1, 2015, https://edition.cnn.com/2014/10/07/business/goal-mapping-career-success/index.html.

88 "World War Two and the Transition to Independence," Country Studies, accessed November 18, 2021, http://countrystudies.us/sri-lanka/21.htm.

89 "A*Star Redeploys Data Storage Institute's Renowned Capabilities in Alignment with National Research and Innovation Strategies," News, A*Star, accessed November 8, 2021,https://www.a-star.edu.sg/News-and-Events/a-star-news/news/press-releases/a-star-redeploys-data-storage-institute-s-renowned-capabilities-in-alignment-with-national-research-and-innovation-strategies-.

90 "Ram Charan Global Adviser to CEOs, Corporate Boards, Bestselling Author," The Industry Leaders, accessed November 8, 2021, https://www.theindustryleaders.org/post/ram-charan-global-adviser-to-ceos-corporate-boards-bestselling-author.

91 "Ram Charan—Business Consultant, Author, CEO Advisor," Ram-Charan, accessed November 9, 2021, https://ram-charan.com/about-ram/.

# ACKNOWLEDGMENTS

I know that most of my colleagues from college may have predicted that I would go on to do a PhD in electrical engineering and saw me since then as a college professor. However, with great insights and suggestions from Dr. Paul Hoole, I started off my career in the industry in Singapore, and that's where I embarked on my journey in leadership. I would like to express my deepest gratitude to Dr. Hoole, who set the foundation on academic research excellence during my undergraduate years and encouraged my industrial career path in later years. That strong foundation made this book possible for me, with over 25 years of leadership experience in large organizations in Asia, the United States, and Europe.

I would like to express my deepest gratitude to all my past and present bosses, peers, subordinates, and other stakeholders with whom I learned, gained experience, and got my leadership skills tested, making it possible to start this book with strong, real-life experiences and academic research. I would like to thank Dr. Hassan Qudrat-Ullah for creating the first interest in me on the research on complexity leadership.

I want to thank my parents for their lifelong courage to go through what they did, raising nine children and becoming my superheroes in life. My gratitude goes to them for starting my foundation with ancient wisdom that eventually led to bridge with modern science, making this book on tackling complexity possible.

I would also like to thank my wife, Sagarika, for taking over all the family commitments all through the hard times, and my daughter, Lawanya, and my son, Mihan, for their continual encouragement and support. They stood by me in good and bad times, making my life easy, challenging life decisions, and making it possible to move around the world. This book is a testimony for my supportive family.

I would like to thank the academic and administrative staff of East China University of Science and Technology School of Business for industrial and academic partnerships that motivated me to expedite getting this book published and sharing my experiences and findings. I would like to thank the excellent team at Book Launchers who have been sharp and precise throughout, making sure this book is launched on time with high quality.

Last, I would like to thank all my colleagues and mentees around the world whom I now feel have given me an opportunity to validate my teachable point of view and leadership point of view, to give excellent feedback, and to see them rising to their true potential.

# INDEX

A320neo  29, 30
A380  13, 49, 197
Accountability  vii, 3, 181
Adapt  ix, 36, 151, 182
Airbus  13, 29, 30, 49, 118, 197
Ancient wisdom  207
Angel Cabrera  71
Apple  145, 146, 167, 205
Aptiv  193
Art of War  88, 202
Average  vii, 18, 108
Behavior  ix, 109
Behavioral leadership  16
Be Here Now  ix, 143, 145
Boeing  vii, 2, 13, 27, 28, 29, 30, 32, 49, 51, 54, 59, 101, 110, 118, 135, 136, 140, 199, 200, 203, 204
Broken Windows Theory  ix, 118

Business unit  14, 57, 114, 129, 155, 185
CEO  2, 11, 13, 22, 23, 28, 30, 48, 51, 52, 61, 62, 63, 96, 101, 110, 127, 134, 135, 136, 138, 140, 145, 167, 193, 200, 204, 206
CFO  54
Change management  168
Chaos  1, 118
Chaotic  33
China  32, 60, 61, 85, 201, 202, 208
Color-blind  192
Commitments  1, 11, 13, 14, 15, 19, 26, 49, 81, 95, 100, 105, 111, 115, 116, 117, 118, 128, 147, 168, 171, 208
Communication  98, 115, 118, 131, 145, 178

Competitive advantage   17, 106, 124
Complex   vii, 25
Complex adaptive systems   5, 25, 27, 59, 175
Complexity   vii, 9, 21, 27, 31, 34, 183
Complicated   20, 21, 32, 33
Confront   122
Confucian theory   87
Consistency   95, 99, 123
Contingency leadership   16
Continuous improvement   134, 166
Conversation   viii, 95
Cost reduction   54, 59
COVID-19   12, 22, 32, 48, 198
Crisis   109, 200
Culp, Larry   134, 135, 204
Culture   203
Customers   116, 166, 201
Cynefin model   31
Danaher   134, 135, 204
Danaher Business System (DBS)   134
Dasa Raja Dhamma   87
Decision   197
Delphi   165, 192, 193
Design   30, 31, 48, 49, 51, 54, 58, 61, 62, 113, 114, 115, 118, 128, 131, 166, 191
Drucker, Peter   18, 82, 202

Edison, Thomas   146
Emergence   viii, 58, 63, 64
Emirates Airlines   13
Enders, Tom   13
Enrico, Roger   138
Escalation   ix, 97, 119, 181
Ethiopian Airlines   29
Excellence   176, 177
Finance   44, 46, 134, 192
Floyd, George   22, 32, 198
Ford   101, 102, 136, 140, 203, 204
General Electric   23, 24, 138, 146
General Motors   47, 102
Great Man Theory   197
Jobs, Steve   144, 145, 146, 194, 204, 205
Habits   x, 175, 176
Hiroo Onoda   74, 75, 202
Immelt, Jeff   23
India   73, 76, 144, 145, 146, 186, 193, 204, 205
Individual change profile   182
Indra Nooyi   138
Innovation   28, 206
Intentions   viii, 99
Interact   viii, 36, 91, 181
Interconnectivity   viii, 31, 44
Internalize   viii, 36, 69, 181
Intimacy   viii, 100
Japan   24, 75, 166
Johnson Electric   95, 96, 189, 193
Knowing yourself   81, 87

# INDEX

Knowledge ix, x, 128, 132, 153, 175, 188, 198

Kodak 166, 167, 206

Kong Fu Tze 87

Leadership vii, viii, ix, x, 7, 15, 16, 18, 52, 76, 84, 95, 97, 127, 128, 131, 137, 138, 146, 176, 193, 197, 198, 203

Leadership point of view 7, 150, 194, 208

Learn ix, 36, 125, 127, 138, 182

Machiavellianism 76, 77

Melrose, Ken 61

Motorola 167

Muilenburg, Dennis 2, 27, 51, 59, 110, 135, 136, 200, 204

Mulally, Alan 101, 140, 203

Nokia 167

Philippines 75

Ram Charan 193, 194, 206

SIILA Model vii, ix, 5, 34, 169

Singapore 165, 186, 191, 192, 202, 207

Snowden, Dave 31

Sri Lanka 72, 186, 191, 194

Switzerland 96, 114, 115, 189, 193

Teachable point of view 182

Toyota 24, 94, 134, 199

Unconscious competence 178, 179

Wang, Patrick 96, 193

Welch, Jack 23, 138, 198, 199

World War II 60, 74, 186, 202

CPSIA information can be obtained
at www.ICGtesting.com
Printed in the USA
LVHW111203050622
720530LV00003B/50/J

9 789811 825552